Remembering MARVIN

Marvin Kaplan: A Prince of Comedy, Creativity, and Kindness

By Ken Rotcop

Remembering Marvin
Marvin Kaplan: A Prince of Comedy, Creativity, and Kindness
by Ken Rotocop

Published in the USA by:
BearManor Media
P O Box 71426
Albany, Georgia 31708
www.bearmanormedia.com

ISBN: 978-1-62933-280-2
BearManor Media, Albany, Georgia
Printed in the United States of America
Cover Design by Daniel J Klein, www.LightInteractiveMedia.com
Book design by Robbie Adkins, www.adkinsconsult.com

All profits from the sale of this book will be forwarded to the Marvin Kaplan-Richard Loring Foundation established to educate aspiring actors and writers in the field of comedy.

It was Marvin's desire to give back to an industry that he loved and to help young people realize their dream.

Marvin had no wife or children. This foundation was to be his legacy to benefit the entertainment industry to which he devoted his life.

Richard Loring was Marvin's music writing partner. He, too, is deceased.

The foundation will also be used to fund scholarships and to pay for tuition and books at Marvin's alma mater, Brooklyn College, for a promising comedian, songwriter, composure, or book writer, as selected by the college.

Memorial gifts may be sent to:
The Kaplan-Loring Foundation
P.O. Box 1577
Burbank, CA 91507

THANKS

There is no way this book would have been written without the help of some of Marvin's friends and relatives.

A big thank you to Carol Egan and her sister, Kathy Peck, who opened up Marvin's house to me.

Thank you to Sara Ballantine for sharing her documentary, Troopers, which featured Marvin.

To Jack Layden for sharing warm remembrance of Marvin.

To Dr. Steven Brown who was too young to really remember Marvin but who took the time to direct me to Carol and Kathy.

To Melissa Gilleece, who was one of the people who put together Marvin's memorial and supplied me with names and information.

To Dan Klein for another great cover.

And finally, to my assistant, Rachel Wolf, for putting up with me, for being there whenever I needed her, for remembering names and places that I've long forgotten, and for typing this manuscript over and over because I prefer to write in a quiet library with a yellow pad and pencil. Soon I will pass the torch to her and she will be a much better writer than I have ever been.

DEDICATED TO
THE ONES I LOVE

This story was told to me by one of my daughter's teachers when she was either in the first, second, or third grade. The teacher, to show the kids how diversified their lives were, asked each of them to tell the class what their fathers did for a living.

One child said her father was a pharmacist, another said her father was a dentist, a third one said her father was a lawyer, and when they got around to my daughter, she said, "My daddy doesn't do anything. He's a writer."

Well this do-nothing father would like to dedicate this book, my fourth, to my children, Kimberly and Alison, my granddaughter Aja, and my two great grandchildren, London Blue and Georgie.

And once again to Tyler.

And, always always, to Connie.

Once Upon a Time in Hollywood...

"Mr. Cukor, Katherine Hepburn on line three."

"Thank you, Hilda."

Cukor hit the button for line three and picked up the phone.

"Hello, Katie."

"George, how are you?"

"Did you get the rewrites?"

"I did. I like 'em. I also like the title *Adam's Rib* better than *Man and Wife*."

"Yeah, we do too. So, Katie, to what do I owe the pleasure of this call?"

"Last night we went to a play over at Charlie Chaplin's theater, I saw an actor. He'd be perfect for the court stenographer in *Adam's Rib*. He's got thick round glasses, talks like he's right out of Brooklyn, and he looks and sounds like a 'shlamiel'."

"Katie, what do you know from 'shlamiel'?"

"But he's sweet. He's got a kind face. And he stole the show. He's got great timing He's very, very funny. And—"

"Alright! Enough already! What are you, his agent?"

"Will you meet him, George?"

"I'll meet him, I'll meet him. What's his name?"

"Kaplan. Marvin Kaplan."

Prologue

I guess it was all because of the Academy Awards.

The "In Memory of..." part where they list all the actors, producers, directors, and office boys who died that year.

But they left out Marvin Kaplan.

Marvin Kaplan!

One of the most beloved actors, famous faces, and voices in all of Hollywood!

And more acting credits than half the names they did mention!

I went through the three stages of anger. First, confused. Did I blink and miss his name? Second, bugged. How dare they not mention Marvin! And the third stage, more bugged! Why do I ever watch that show? It's long, boring, and I never win anyway.

Well, actually that's not quite true. I had sat through three different long and boring shows and won the Writers Guild Award, the NAACP Image Award, and the Neil Simon Award. All for my writing and producing.

But back to Marvin Kaplan.

I emailed my publisher and told him I was furious the Academy left out Marvin and wanted to write a book about this wonderful actor, writer, and friend. Maybe the Academy forgot him, but his fans won't!

The publisher sent me a contract.

And that's how this biography came to be.

TABLE OF CONTENTS

EVERY TUESDAY EVENING

I don't know how many years I knew Marvin. Oh, I had seen him, of course, in *It's A Mad, Mad, Mad, Mad World* and *The Great Race* and dozens of TV shows. I may not have known his name, but with those big, round, metal-rimmed glasses and that Brooklyn accent, I certainly remembered that sad-sack face.

But I really got to know Marvin when he joined my screenwriter's workshop at my house. Every Tuesday, for years, Marvin was there.

And in the last years, when his friend Steve Carter would have to wheel Marvin up my driveway, pages of a new script sitting on Marvin's lap, Marvin was there.

And when his eyesight began to fail him behind those thick, thick glasses and his hearing dimmed, Marvin was still there, in his regular chair, in my living room, every Tuesday evening. And every Tuesday he'd bring in new pages of a screenplay or a theatrical play he would be writing.

Besides the workshop, we'd do lunch or we'd talk on the phone regularly.

We'd talk movies, or theater, or his scripts. He'd go to New York yearly and would tell me about all the Broadway plays he had seen. What was good and why it was good, and what was bad and why it was bad.

We'd talk about *Watch Out for Slick*, a movie he produced that he wrote in our workshop. While they were shooting, he worried about the director, the actors, the locations, and the cameraman.

He was a worrier. But never on the set, and never to the actors or the crew.

But to me he would talk about what was good with the film and why it was good, and what was bad and why it was bad.

I loved those conversations with Marvin. I was the teacher. He was my student. But it was I who learned so much from him.

Marvin loved to write. He loved to sing. He loved to perform. And he loved to talk.

Boy, could he talk.

I began taking notes but never thinking I would someday be writing this remembrance.

Oh, yeah, and he loved to eat.

There wasn't a delicatessen in the San Fernando Valley we didn't visit at one time or another.

This book is not a biography. It's stories. Stories Marvin told. Stories others told about Marvin.

"Did I ever tell you the time I..." And he'd be off remembering another moment in his life.

I'm going to miss those moments.

Marvin going on an interview (c1948).

BYE BYE BROOKLYN

Marvin left Brooklyn in 1947 to come to Hollywood. "Up to that time, I wanted to be either a playwright because I loved Broadway plays, or write for radio because I loved all the old detective shows and *Suspense* and *Lights Out*."

He went to USC to get a master's degree in theater. One day, William DeMille, a professor at the school, called Marvin into his office.

"Mr. Kaplan, I think it's time for you to drop out of school."

"Huh?"

"You've taken every theater course we offer. It's time to go out and get a job."

"A job?"

"In one of the theaters here in town."

"But I don't know anyone. Who would hire me?"

DeMille thought a second. "Offer your services as an assistant stage manager. Work for nothing if you have to. But go see what actors do to writers' lines. Go see why writers get heartburn!"

Because he had no car, Marvin walked a couple of miles to a small theater called The Actor's Lab.

"Sorry, Kaplan, but we're all guys that went to UCLA together and we just don't hire outside people."

Marvin started to leave when the guy called out, "Why don't you try the Circle Theater over on El Centro. Maybe you'll get lucky."

Marvin took the bus to the Circle Theater.

"I've just come from the Actor's Lab and—"

The young man stopped Marvin. "We were about to give up on you. Glad you're here."

They were not expecting Marvin. They were expecting someone else!

They offered Marvin the job as the stage manager. Not the assistant stage manager, the stage manager.

Marvin grabbed the job and started working immediately.

The next day, someone came to the stage door and started looking around as if he'd never been there before.

Marvin greeted him. "Can I help you?"

"Yes. I'm the new stage manager."

Some of the other members of the Circle Theater came over to help Marvin out.

"Sorry, but when you didn't show up yesterday..."

And they made some excuse to blow the new guy off.

Marvin kept his job.

The director at the theater was Charlie Chaplin. Yes, *the* Charlie Chaplin.

Marvin, the stage manager, watched rehearsals and listened to everything Chaplin said or demonstrated. And he learned.

"I loved Chaplin." Marvin once told me over lunch at Fromin's Deli, "Whatever he said, I later would write it down, then memorize it."

He remembered Chaplin blocking a scene. He turned to Marvin and asked how many steps did it take for an actor to cross the stage.

Marvin didn't know. But if you asked him fifty-years later, he'd tell you! He never forgot.

Two other things that Marvin jotted down that Chaplin said:

"Always try to tinge your comedy with a little sadness." And, "If what you're doing is funny, don't be funny doing it."

At Christmas, the company decided to perform *Aladdin and his Wonderful Lamp*. The cast was dressed in Middle Eastern costumes. They had a live monkey playing the part of a live monkey. And Charlie Chaplin's son, Sidney, played the genie.

Charlie Chaplin was in the audience, but not seated. He was too hyper, too nervous to watch his son. So, during the entire performance, he paced around the theater.

The audience, of course, was not watching the play, they were all watching the great Charlie Chaplin walking, pacing, stifling his laughter at different parts in the play so as not to disturb the actors or the audience.

And Marvin? They actually gave him a part in the play.

"I wore dark, Egyptian makeup. I did not wear my glasses. At different times in the show, I'm supposed to hold up cards for the audience. But without my glasses I couldn't see anything, let alone the writing on the cards.

"So, some of the cards I held upside down, and some I held sideways. The audience was laughing, but I didn't know why. I thought maybe the monkey was doing something funny behind me!

"When I found out later they were laughing at me, I felt bad that I had screwed it up.

"Charlie Chaplin came backstage after the show to congratulate his son Sidney and the rest of the cast and crew.

"We all stood around this great actor, waiting for his critique. He looked at all of us, smiled, and said, 'Sidney, you were good. And the monkey, he was good too.' He then looked at me. 'But you, young man, playing the nearsighted Nubian slave, you really cracked me up!'

"It was one of the greatest compliments I ever got!"

Chaplin put Marvin in charge of the monkey and the monkey followed Marvin around everywhere he went.

Marvin was really broke in those days. He was so excited when he got his first paycheck from the theater. At last he could afford a hot meal. Except it never happened. The monkey ate the check!

✖ ✖ ✖

Now a full-fledged member of the Circle Theater, Marvin auditioned for the next play, a French farce by Moliere, *The Doctor in Spite of Himself*. He read for the part of Lucas. Marvin called it "a damn roll."

When he read all his French lines with his Brooklyn accent, the director couldn't stop laughing.

"Mr. Kaplan, you are so wrong for this play, so badly suited for French farce, you're hired!"

All the other actors auditioning that day applauded! And laughed!

When the play opened, some reviews said Marvin was the hit of the show, while other reviews said he was badly cast.

But the only critic that really mattered was soon to enter the theater and change Marvin's life forever.

And So It Begins…

Somewhere between the third or fourth week of the show, Katherine Hepburn came backstage.

The first time I heard this story was at our annual Writers Workshop Christmas party where Marvin stood up in front of all of the writers and their spouses and entertained us easily for thirty to forty minutes.

"One night we had about ten people in the house. Things were not looking so good. After the show everybody was kind of down in the dumps. Suddenly, everyone in the cast got real quiet. I looked up to see what was happening, and there was Miss Hepburn walking straight towards me.

"She was absolutely stunning, gorgeous. At that time, she was in her mid-40's. She wore no makeup.

"'You're Marvin Kaplan, aren't you?' I was so flustered it took all my strength just to nod yes.

"'Have you done a lot of work?'

"No, this is my first job."

"'Well, Mr. Kaplan, you were awfully good.'

"I wanted to thank her, but instead, and it was very forward of me, I blurted out, 'I hope you don't think I'm being impertinent, but you remind me of my sister. You both have red hair and freckles.

"To which she said, 'Yes, it's this damn sun! Nice meeting you, Mr. Kaplan.'

"And with that, she left."

The next day, when Marvin came to the theater for rehearsals, there was a note on a bulletin board for him to call MGM.

"I had applied to MGM for a job as a page boy, so I figured that's what the message was about," he told me one afternoon. "But I was wrong. It was a George Cukor's office calling. They told me I had a 3:00 interview.

"I immediately took a bus home, dressed in my favorite and only suit, and took a taxi to Culver City. I got to MGM with five minutes to spare! The guard had my name on his pass list and pointed me to the talent department.

"They took one look at me and thought I was the new bookkeeper. I mean, in those days, they only hired tall handsome men, and I wasn't tall. But I told them I had an appointment with Mr. Cukor.

"So they sent me to the Irving Thalberg Building. And there I met George Cukor.

"'You have an agent, Mr. Kaplan?' asked Cukor."

"Uh, no."

"You do now."

"I do?"

"Katy Hepburn says she saw you in a play last night."

"Yes, she did."

"She thinks you're wonderful."

All I could think of is that I wished my mother could have been sitting in that room and heard Mr. Cukor.

"Katy Hepburn thinks your wonderful."

Oh, how my mother would have "kveled" (Yiddish for "being proud").

"She wants me to give you a part in our new movie."

The movie was written by Garson Kanin and Ruth Gordon, and called, *Man and Wife*. But when Spencer Tracy and Katherine Hepburn signed on and some changes were made on the script, they decided to change the title to *Adam's Rib*.

Marvin would play a court stenographer taking testimony in shorthand.

Cukor studied Marvin for a moment, as if picturing him in the part. "Your part is to repeat this very gut-wrenching emotional testimony in a dull, flat voice."

Said Marvin quickly, "I have a dull, flat voice."

Cukor winced. "I noticed. Good day, Mr. Kaplan. We'll be in touch."

End of meeting. Beginning of Marvin Kaplan's movie career! It was 1949, and Marvin was twenty-two.

MEYER MISHKIN

That afternoon, Marvin returned to the theater to rehearse the Moliere play that was in its third or fourth week. Why was Marvin rehearsing? Because many in the cast thought his performance wasn't any good.

Here he had just been hired to act in a Tracy-Hepburn movie but the theater people weren't happy with his performance!

He did have one friend in the cast, though. Gregg Martell had brought his agent, Meyer Mishkin, to watch Marvin's work.

Marvin told Gregg about Hepburn and his meeting with George Cukor.

"Think Mr. Mishkin would represent me?" Marvin asked Martell.

"Give him a call," said Martell.

Marvin called and Mishkin signed him to an agent-actor's contract.

And the first thing Mishkin did was call Cukor and tell him Marvin was turning down *Adam's Rib*!

Marvin's heart stopped beating.

"Mr. Mishkin! What are you doing?!"

Mishkin winked at Marvin. "I'm negotiating."

In 1949, pay scale for day actors was $55 a day.

Marvin thought that was great! "I felt that I should pay them," he told me.

But Mishkin had another idea. He told Marvin that if he started for $55 a day it would be almost impossible to get more for his next picture.

"Once you work for $55, you're forever known as a $55 actor. That's the way the business works."

"But..." protested Marvin.

"I'm gonna get you $75 a day. Hey, you're Katherine Hepburn's protege, that's gotta be worth something! At least an extra $20 a day!"

Mishkin got Marvin one day's work at Universal on the movie *Francis The Talking Mule*. It was to shoot before *Adam's Rib*.

Mishkin sold Universal on the fact that Marvin was this "hot new actor" being featured in a Tracy-Hepburn movie.

Universal would pay Marvin $75 for one day's work, if they hired him after interviewing him.

Marvin took a bus to Universal Studios.

The interview began.

"Mr. Kaplan, where did you serve in the army?"

"I didn't. I was 4-F."

"Well then, did you ever go to med school?"

"I took pre-med and I failed."

It was Marvin's innocence and Brooklyn accent to the questions that had those in the room giggling.

The part Marvin was up for was an Army doctor. He figured he blew the audition. What he didn't know was they had seen him in the Moliere play and the job was his even before he walked in the door!

When he called Mishkin later to tell him he blew the audition, Meyer laughed. "They loved you! They think you're hysterical! You got the job! And your price is now $75 for the day!"

Here's Marvin's part for which he got $75. Remember, he's wearing a white smock because he's supposed to be an Army doctor. His scene is with Donald O'Connor.

MARVIN
Tell me, Sterling, is it just one mule that talks
to you, or do all the mules talk to you?

O'CONNOR
Just Francis.

MARVIN
Francis?

And that was Marvin's $75 speaking role. But wait! There's more!

Marvin really liked Donald O'Connor. He liked that O'Connor shook hands with all the actors and the crew and greeted everyone who came on the set.

"That's the way they did it in the old days," Marvin told me when we took a break from my workshop.

When O'Connor saw Marvin for the first time he said to the director, "This kid's gonna crack me up!"

Marvin didn't know what O'Connor was talking about. Then Marvin noticed that when he did his scenes (he had the one with O'Connor and another one without dialogue), everyone had handkerchiefs in their mouths to keep from laughing.

But Marvin thought otherwise. "I thought that they thought I was so terrible that they wanted to vomit!"

Marvin's second shot was for him to run into the Army hospital. They put tape on the floor so that he'd hit his mark faster. They did a take. The director told Marvin he was too slow getting to his mark. Marvin was afraid they'd fire him. So the next take he bolted into the room after knocking over a nurse and plowing through one of the patients. He was so fast the cameraman couldn't keep up with him!

After a number of takes that left Marvin breathless, they got the shot.

That evening he called Mishkin.

"Meyer, I'm going back to New York. I'm a lousy actor and they all hated me. I hope I didn't ruin their movie. Meyer, at $75, I was overpaid."

Meyer begged him not to leave town till he spoke to the people at Universal. He called Marvin the next day. They had watched the dailies.

"Marvin, they loved you! On the phone, they were laughing!"

"All I had was one line."

"I've never, in all my years, heard such a reaction."

"So I shouldn't go back to Brooklyn?"

"Are you crazy?! *Adam's Rib* starts next week, and when I told them you got a featured part in Francis they raised you to $250 a week. What do ya think of that?!"

Marvin mumbled, "A featured part? I only had one line!"

"It's called negotiating, Marvin. Negotiating!"

ADAM'S RIB

So Marvin went to work on *Adam's Rib*. Marvin liked George Cukor a lot. Said he was one of the nicest men he ever met. Cukor thanked Marvin personally for being in the picture. Cukor was a top director, and one of his first features in 1932 was a film called *A Bill of Divorcement*. There was a young lady he wanted to star in the film, an actress he had discovered. But the studio didn't want her. Said she was too boyish, that no one would believe her as a leading lady.

Cukor fought for her. The studio eventually caved in. Her name? Katherine Hepburn.

It was the first day on the courtroom set, and Hepburn told Marvin, "You're the court stenographer, so this is where you'll sit for the next two weeks." According to Marvin, Hepburn always looked after him while he was working there.

And one day she saved him from being fired.

His dressing room was at least the length of two football fields from the sound stage, and Marvin, cherubic face sweating, eyeglasses steamed, was racing as fast as his chubby legs would take him from the sound stage to his dressing room, only to literally bump into Hepburn.

"Joining our Olympic team, Marvin?"

"Mr. Cukor wants to do a close-up of me."

"So instead you're running away?"

"I have the wrong suit. It's supposed to be the same suit that was in the shot yesterday. I'm sorry, Miss Hepburn, I gotta run."

The way Marvin told me the story, Cukor was upset that Marvin was holding up the shot!

Hepburn sidled up to Cukor. "The boy was running to his dressing room to change outfits. I don't think he's ever run so fast or so far in his whole life. I'm afraid he must have keeled over and died. Poor thing never got his close-up."

Cukor couldn't get angry with Hepburn. "She got me the job and she saved my job," Marvin reminisced.

"The one who could have been fired was Molly Kent, the script girl. It was her job to make sure I wore the same outfit as the day before. She goofed, and I ran the race of my life! She thanked me at least a half a dozen times."

According to Marvin, the clown of the cast was Spencer Tracy. He loved to play practical jokes on everybody.

Including Marvin.

At the end of the courtroom scene, Marvin congratulated Miss Hepburn but didn't get to Mr. Tracy. When Marvin swung a door open to leave, he accidentally smacked Tracy right in the back. Tracy let out a howl and crumbled to the floor. Marvin thought he had killed him.

Marvin got on his knees, apologized like crazy, and felt sick in the pit of his stomach.

Tracy opened his eyes, grinned, and said, "That's all right, kid. Just don't do it again."

Tracy had whacked his hand against the door to make the thump. The door never touched his back. And he wasn't dead.

✖ ✖ ✖

Only one person ever got back at Tracy, remembered Marvin. Hope Emerson played the circus lady billed as "the strongest lady in the world." In one scene, she lifted Tracy (who is harnessed to an invisible wire) and held him high above her head with one hand. While he was up there, Tracy kept giving her a hard time. She got pissed, pulled her hand away, and left him to dangle in mid-air.

"Gotcha, Spencer!" Everyone laughed and applauded.

✖ ✖ ✖

When the picture wrapped, they had a cast party at Mr. Cukor's very elegant home. Hepburn personally called Marvin and invited him. Only he and one other supporting actor received invites. Marvin hitched a ride with one of the assistants.

Marvin said the next scene was right out of a movie.

To get to the house, one walked through a huge, beautiful court-yard. Hepburn was wearing a long red dress. She walked the length of the courtyard, past groups of important, well-dressed people, to greet Marvin.

"I'm so glad you could come," she welcomed him, touching his hand with hers.

He said he nearly fainted. Marvin's first Hollywood crush.

It was never recorded if she felt the same.

✖ ✖ ✖

Marvin remembered going to the Egyptian Theatre on Holly-wood Boulevard to watch a preview of *Adam's Rib*. Evidently it was a terrible shock for Marvin to see himself on the big screen.

"I wanted to tear myself off the screen," he said. "I was such an amateur compared to Tracy and Hepburn and Judy Holiday.

"But the audience laughed at my scene! They liked it!"

He couldn't help but think about his parents, and Brooklyn, and as a kid writing little plays and performing them in the house or at camp.

Back then, who knew?

Marvin's high school graduation picture.

Growing Up

Marvin's father, Isidor, was a doctor. The family lived at 537 Bedford Avenue in Brooklyn. It was always assumed Marvin, being the only boy (he had two sisters), would follow in his father's footsteps and go into medicine.

But from the time he could read, Marvin was addicted to the movies. He kept track of all the movie stars. Collected their pictures. He could recite the credits of Clark Gable, Shirley Temple, Joan Crawford, Fred Astaire, and all the stars of the 30s.

Marvin's uncle, Robert Rothman, owned a drugstore where Marvin, as a teenager, worked as a soda-jerk.

"Marvin holds a record," remembered Rothman. "Because all Marvin thought about was going to the movies, or reading the store's movie magazines, or collecting cards with movie stars' pictures, that instead of making malteds and egg creams, he was breaking glasses. Of all the soda-jerks I hired over the years, none, combined, broke as many glasses as Marvin!"

Marvin went to Public School No. 16, Junior High 15. Eastern District High School, and on to Brooklyn College.

At Brooklyn College, Marvin got a job as a reporter for the school newspaper. One of his assignments was to go to the campus theater and watch a rehearsal of Shakespeare's *Taming of the Shrew*, whch they would be performing that night, and write a review.

Marvin got to the theater and the actors, all Brooklyn College theater majors, were sitting around and not rehearsing. It seemed that they just found out one of the guys had to suddenly drop out of school and they would have to run the rehearsal without him. And somewhere at this late date get a replacement.

"Did he have the lead?" Marvin asked the director.

"Not exactly." The director looked young 19-year-old Marvin over. "In fact, his part doesn't have any lines. You wanna know something?" The director had a brilliant idea. "You could be a perfect substitute!"

"But I don't know how to act."

"You don't have to."

"But I came to write a review."

"What better way to review a play than right up on the stage!"

So Marvin broke into show business by playing the back half of a horse suit on stage for all performances.

Is it possible that it may have been there, bent over, his arms wrapped around the guy bent over in front of him, the horse's costume draped over both of them, that Marvin, playing the rear-end of a horse, was maybe just a little bit, bit by the acting bug?

Marvin's older sister, Elinore, had her own law office and, after college, hired Marvin as a law clerk. That job lasted as long as the soda-jerk job because Marvin was determined to go to Hollywood and to do graduate work at the University of Southern California. Despite his acting debut, he was determined to be a playwright. Not a doctor like his father wanted, not a pharmacist like his uncle wanted, not a lawyer like his sister wanted, but someone who writes stories for radio or the theater.

"He'll starve," said his father. "He'll starve," said his uncle. "He'll starve," said his sister.

They were wrong.

Marvin's graduation picture from Brooklyn College.

THE REFORMER AND THE REDHEAD

After small roles in *Adam's Rib* and *Keys to the City*, Marvin was cast in MGM's romantic comedy *The Reformer and the Redhead*. The movie starred husband and wife June Alison and Dick Powell, and gave Marvin a significant role in the story.

While there was buzz in the movie colony about young Marvin's work in his first few small but distinctive roles, nobody outside Hollywood knew his name. But when *The Reformer and the Redhead* was sneak previewed on the West Coast, over 90 percent of the cards turned in by the preview audience commented on Marvin and expressed interest in seeing him in more films.

Suddenly, Marvin was a Hollywood celebrity!

And even though Marvin had come to Los Angeles to write for movies and the theater, he had no time, so busy was he acting.

I Can Get It for You
Wholesale

After the success of *The Reformer and The Redhead*, Daryl Zanuck hired Marvin for a part in *I Can Get It for You Wholesale*, starring Susan Hayward and Don Dailey. It was 1951.

The director, Michael Gordon, who had directed Cyrano de Bergeran, went to see Zanuck.

"Mr. Zanuck, I have a problem."

"Oh? Something wrong, Michael?"

"It's that Marvin Kaplan. He is absolutely wrong for Arnold Fisher. I want to replace him."

"Replace him?"

"He looks wrong. He sounds wrong. His concept of the character is wrong."

"Did you see any of the dailies of *The Reformer and the Redhead*?"

"No," said Gordon. "Why?"

"The kid is brilliant. I'm telling you, when he's on the screen you can't take your eyes off him."

Gordon was stuck and didn't know what to say.

Zanuck ended the conversation with, "I want that kid to play the part. Period."

Marvin worked the first day of shooting and got a call from Meyer Mishkin, his agent.

"Marvin, Sol Siegel wants to talk to you."

Sol Siegel was the producer of the movie. Zanuck was the head of the studio, Twentieth Century Fox.

Marvin was terrified when he went to Siegel's office.

"Sit down, Marvin."

"You wanted to see me, Mr. Siegel?"

"We looked at the dailies. Not good."

Marvin was now fighting for his job. "I agree," he said. "Mr. Gordon sees the character totally different than I see him. And ... he's right, absolutely right."

"So, what should we do?"

Marvin went on to explain, "Mr. Gordon wants me to play Arnold like he's another Sammy Glick, a very opportunistic, aggressive kid. I didn't see it that way. Mr. Gordon thinks Arnold is only dating the boss' daughter to advance his career.

"My interpretation is totally different."

"Shouldn't you be listening to your director? To get his take on the character?"

"Mr. Siegel, just hear me out. I felt my character, Arnold, asked her out because he was lonely and she was the only girl his age working in the company. It's just a different take. But if he wants Sammy Glick, I'll give him Sammy Glick."

Siegel sighed. He hated these kinds of meetings.

"Alright, Marvin. Get back to work."

They scrapped the footage from the first day and started over. Marvin played it Gordon's way, but it was too late. The damage

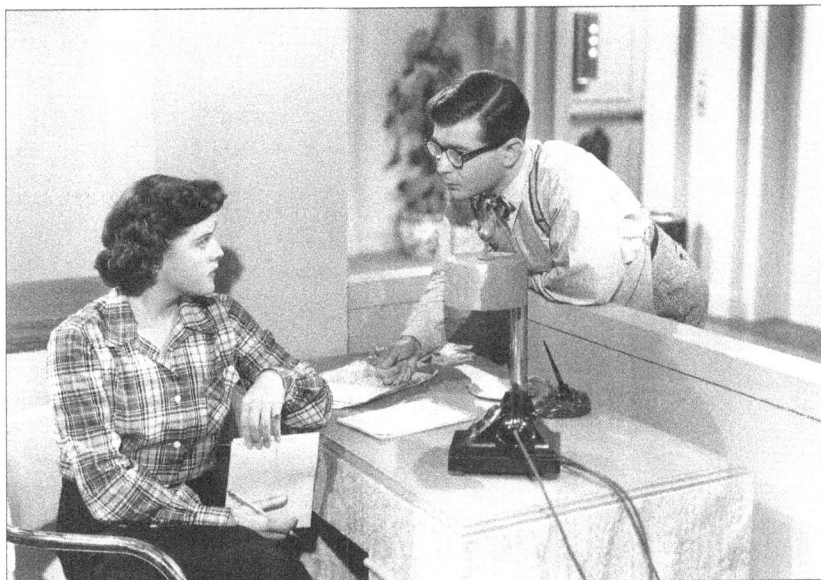

Marvin with actress Barbara Whiting on the set of I Can Get It for You Wholesale *(1951).*

had been done. By Marvin having gone to Sol Siegel, even though Siegel had called for the meeting, Gordon felt Marvin betrayed him, that Marvin had gone behind Gordon's back. From that moment on, Gordon treated Marvin like dirt. It was Sam Jaffe who finally explained to Marvin why Gordon was bullying him.

"Marvin," Jaffe started, "you're it, boychick."

"What do you mean 'I'm it'?"

"Gordon needs a patsy. Someone he can push around, bully. He isn't going to bully Susan Hayward, she would have him fired. If he bullied Dan Daily, Daily would beat him to a pulp and put him in the hospital. George Sanders? No one bullies George Sanders.

"And me," concluded Sam Jaffe, "He wouldn't dare bully me because I'm too lovable!

"So, Marvin, you're it. Sorry."

And so, while Marvin loved everyone in the cast, his life was made miserable by the director. He made Marvin do take after take, which others thought unnecessary. In rehearsals, he was constantly telling Marvin he wasn't doing it right. Other times he would completely ignore Marvin as if Marvin was not part of the cast.

Years later, Marvin told me he ran into Gordon. Gordon put his hand on Marvin's shoulder. "Gee, Marvin, it's really great to see you. I must say your work is extraordinary. How come we haven't worked together again? We've got to find something for the both of us!"

Marvin, who I never heard swear, said to me, "The sunuvabitch completely forgot how he had treated me. Me work with him?! Never! When *I Can Get It for You Wholesale* was released, I went to a theater to see it. Part way through I left. It was just too hard to sit through it because it reminded me how miserable I had been during the shooting."

Marvin with Susan Hayward in I Can Get It for You Wholesale *(1951)*

It's a Mad, Mad, Mad, Mad World

In 1963, Myer Mishkin, Marvin's agent, sent him a script titled *Mad, Mad, Mad, Mad World*. It was to be a zany comedy directed by Stanley Kramer, and to star or feature every living comic in Hollywood!

"Your part," said Mishkin, "will be an assistant to Edward Everett Horton."

When the script arrived at Marvin's house, he practically got a hernia trying to lift it.

"It was thicker than the Manhattan phonebook," Marvin told me years later at Jerry's Deli in Woodland Hills.

"While the part wasn't large or particularly funny, I was thrilled and honored just to be in the company of such great comedians."

A few days later Mishkin was on the phone again.

"Jackie Mason is out," announced the agent.

"What do you mean 'out'?" asked Marvin.

"He gave Stanley Kramer his night club schedule and there were too many conflicts."

"Couldn't they shoot around him?" asked Marvin. "After all, he's a funny man."

"Mr. Kramer came up with a better idea. He fired him. Look, Marvin, they need someone fast. You still got the whole script?"

"Of course. It's sitting on the floor in the living room. I'm waiting for three of my friends to come over to help me lift it onto my desk!"

"Save your shtick for the movie," said Mishkin chuckling. "Read the gas station scene."

An hour later, Marvin called Mishkin back.

"Myer, are you crazy?! I can't do that part!"

"Marvin, what are you talking about?!"

"There are stunts. I get thrown through a plate glass window! A wall of a building falls on top of me! I have to throw big, heavy oil drums!"

"Marvin, listen to me. Whatever stunts your partner does, you'll do. That's the deal."

"Who's my partner?"

"Arnold Stang."

Arnold Stang, besides being a funny-looking, squeaky voiced actor, was short, skinny, and a 98-pound weakling. Marvin was suddenly feeling better.

"Arnold is the biggest coward in America. If he consents to do a stunt, I'll consent to do a stunt!" Marvin knew that somehow Arnold would get out of doing his own stunts.

What Marvin did not know was that the third guy in the scene was an ex-Marine who insisted the three do their own stunts. His name was Jonathan Winters!

So that is how Marvin got to be in the garage scene in *Mad, Mad, Mad, Mad World*, a scene that has gone down in the annals of slapstick cinema as a classic moment in film.

Now Marvin and Arnold were not in any of Jonathan Winter's other scenes, so they would sit in the desert watching Winters work. And they would talk in hushed voices to each other.

"Maybe he'll get hurt," Arnold whispered to Marvin. "And they'll have to bring in stuntmen to do his stunts and our stunts."

"You're wishing for Johnny to get hurt?!" Marvin whispered back.

"Not badly. Not like a broken bone. But just bad enough so he'd need a stunt man."

And wouldn't you know it?! Rehearsing for all the chaos and choreography needed for the garage sequence, Jonathan Winters sprained his back!

Marvin and Arnold looked at each other. They fought trying not to giggle out loud. They knew that Winters was no longer able to do his own stunts. If Winters got a stunt man, that meant Arnold and Marvin would get one too!

It was not easy finding a stunt man for Arnold since, on his tippy-toes, he stood only five-foot-three inches tall. They hired

Marvin on set with Arnold Stang in It's a Mad, Mad, Mad, Mad World
(1963).

Janos Prohaska who, in jungle movies, played chimps, monkeys, and small apes.

The thing with Arnold was that he had no chin and no shoulders. whereas Janos had huge shoulders. So, they actually built up Arnold's shoulders so he'd look as good as his stunt man!

Marvin's stunt man, Bill Maxwell, was very handsome, but thin as a rail. First, they put Marvin's thick glasses on Maxwell and he couldn't see his hand in front of his face. In fact, Marvin said Maxwell, wearing the glasses, walked right into a tree. They also kept putting padding on the stunt man because Marvin was chubby and they wanted Maxwell to look chubby. But Marvin kept taking the padding out because he wanted to look thin!

"Look at those series of shots," said Marvin. "That's Prohaska and Maxwell doing all the work. Thank god, because Arnold and I would've gotten killed!"

"And the funny thing is Arnold was already in pain. He had broken his left wrist just before we started shooting. And he was a lefty. So they gave him big mechanic's gloves to wear and a big wrench to hold in his bad hand. When you watch the scene, notice Arnold is wearing white gloves. Whenever he had an action to do he always did it with his right hand. It wasn't easy because it wasn't his strong hand. He couldn't even brush his teeth with that hand.

"The whole cast was great. Nice people, all of them. Milton Berle, Sid Caesar, Mickey Rooney, Carl Reiner, Phil Silvers. Too many to mention.

"I liked 'em all. Except Buddy Hackett. He had a real mean streak. One day he threw a knife at me. Not a fake knife. Not a prop. A real, sharp, pointed knife! It landed between my fingers and stuck to the couch I was leaning against. He thought he was being funny.

"Another time he took my glasses off while I was wearing them and rubbed his thumbs and fore fingers all over the lenses then put them back on my face. Of course they were so smudged I couldn't see out of them. He thought that was funny, too.

"No, I did not like Buddy Hackett."

It's a Mad, Mad, Mad, Mad World took two years to make and ran in the theaters almost that long. (Actually, the original was three hours, seventeen minutes.) It was shot in thirty California locations, many in the desert, many in heat over 105.

Marvin was fortunate to share one of the few air-conditioned trailers on location with Winters.

"We would play a game in the trailer," recalled Marvin. "It was called, 'Who are you today, Jonathan?' He would improvise or mimic or mime, sometimes up to an hour, making up characters as he went along. And this was just to kill time waiting to be called out to shoot the next scene."

Marvin once told me there were two comedy geniuses in his life. One was Jonathan Winters. The other Charlie Chaplin.

Here, for those who never saw it or for those who want to remember, is the entire gas station scene from *It's a Mad, Mad, Mad, Mad World*.

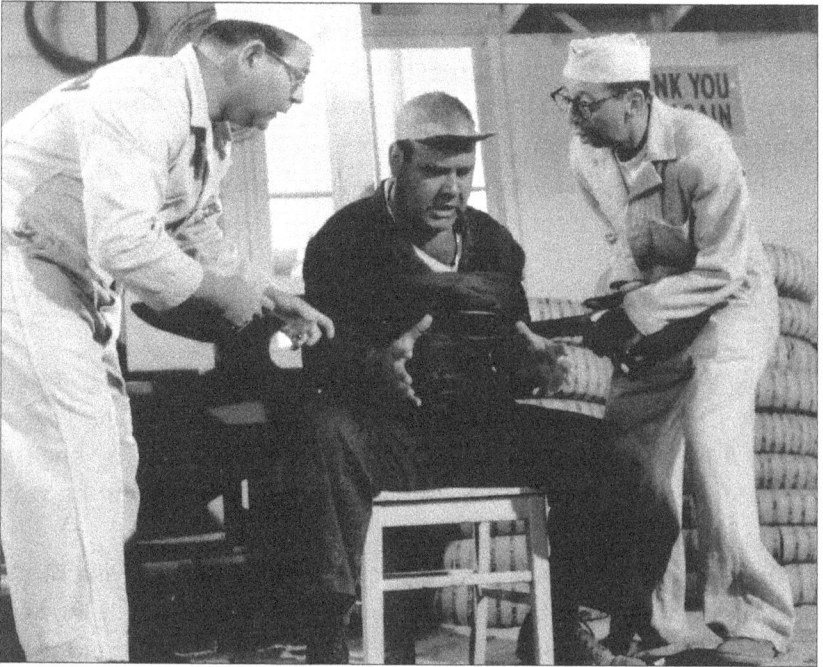

Marvin on set with Jonathan Winters and Arnold Stang in It's a Mad Mad Mad Mad World *(1963)*.

The Classic
Gas Station Scene

Phil Silvers stops at a gas station to fill up his car when Jonathan Winters, sore as hell, comes wheeling up on a bicycle. Silvers had dumped him earlier. Silvers tells the two gas station attendants, played by Marvin and Arnold, that Winters is a homicidal lunatic who just escaped from an asylum.

In truth, both Winters and Silvers are part of a group of strangers who are traveling across Southern California to get to $350,000 buried in Santa Rosita. (Today the money would be worth close to three million.)

Winters chases Silvers around the car, tackles Silvers, rips off the passenger side door, and throws him against a gas pump that keeps going "kaching" every time Winters shoves Silvers' head against the pump.

Winters then grabs two new tires and pummels Silvers with them until Arnold hits Winters over the head with a tire iron, knocking him out.

Silvers tells the boys to tie Winters up and that he will have the men in white jackets come by with a straight jacket.

In the garage, they wrap tape around Winters, securing him to a chair. As Winters is about to bust out of the tape, Arnold swings a huge monkey wrench, misses Winters' head, and smashes Marvin on the arm.

Breaking out of the tape, his momentum springs Winters crashing through the wall between the garage and the office.

Sticking his head through the hole in the wall, first Arnold, then Marvin, clobber Winters by smashing bottles over his head.

This pisses Winters off. He comes through the hole, chasing the boys.

Marvin throws an oil drum that misses Winters who throws Arnold against the garage door and throws Marvin against a wall.

Winters then picks up Arnold and, meaning to toss him out the window, actually knocks over a wall leading to the outside.

The boys race to the stand-alone restrooms, Marvin going into and locking the men's room, Arnold going in and locking the ladies' room.

Winters knocks over the whole thing and continues to chase the boys, who miraculously have escaped the toilets.

Back in the office, Winters throws Marvin through a window, knocking over a patio overhang.

Winters then picks up Arnold, lies him on his belly on an old-fashioned Coca Cola chest-type cooler, and rolls Arnold and the cooler through another window, hitting a post that knocks down another part of the overhang.

The boys then charge Winters using an axel of a car like a battering ram. Of course they miss Winters, and send shelves with oil cans flying in all directions.

Next, the boys, running out of ingenious weapons, go back to throwing oil drums at Winters.

Winters then charges them with a car's motor that is hanging on an overhead pulley. He misses the boys but manages to crash the motor into a wall, knocking the wall over.

The boys then roll under an opening under the garage door. Winters follows, then throws the boys through the garage door back into the garage.

When Winters spies the boys' tow truck, he gets in and backs it into the garage, knocking over all the existing walls plus a water tower next to the gas station.

He then drives off just as the last standing wall, of its own volition, crumbles, breaking into a million pieces.

The gas station sequence was over. The cast and crew standing behind the camera applauded and whistled.

Except somebody goofed.

The gas station was demolished before all the close-up scenes had been filmed. The whole gas station, garage, and office had to be rebuilt overnight. A little mistake that cost the production, in those days, over $100,000!

The scene is considered a classic.

Was it funny? Zany? Crazy? Stupid?

Yes.

With the voices of Allen Jenkins as Top Cat and Marvin as Choo Choo. (1961-1962).

Top Cat

It's not known how many hundreds of pet owners named their kittens Choo-Choo after the lovable cat in the animated TV series *Top Cat*.

He was a pink cat, always wore a white turtleneck, had a black-tipped tail, lived in a fire house, and spoke with the Brooklynese voice of Marvin Kaplan. In fact, when Marvin met Joe Barbera of Hanna-Barbera fame and asked him what kind of voice he should use for Choo-Choo, Barbera simply said, "Yours."

In a press release, Bill Hanna said, "We chose alley cats for our heroes because they have real living problems, problems that people can easily identify themselves with. *Top Cat* and his friends have a constant struggle to survive, but they love their freedom."

Choo-Choo was devoted to Top Cat, who was constantly giving "Chooch" jobs to do. And Choo-Choo would run off with great enthusiasm to please Top Cat, though he never had a clue as to what he was doing or why.

But not everybody loved the lovable pink alley cat. For when it came to females, poor Choo-Choo was either tongue-tied, painfully shy, or reduced to stammering. Poor Chooch was always falling for someone out of his class. And he was always getting turned down.

Some say Top Cat and his friends were inspired by the Dead End Kids, a bunch of street kids from a series of B movies started in the 1930s. Other sources claim the inspiration for Top Cat was "Bilko," a sit-com about the Army starring Phil Silvers.

One of Marvin's closest friends in the cast was Maurice Gosfield, who had played Pvt. Doberman on Sgt. Bilko.

"He was the funniest man I ever worked with. I absolutely worshipped him!" I swear Marvin's eyes sparkled when he remembered Maurice Doberman.

The show ran from 1961-1962, had 30 episodes, and was shown on ABC. Today, *Top Cat* plays in 50 countries around the world.

Here's what Marvin had to say about *Top Cat*.

"It was a different kind of cartoon. It was very intelligent. Nowadays it's all grunts and people falling off mountains. Very violent.

"*Top Cat* was all very good humor. And adult humor. And we even had an adult time slot, a night time slot.

"Joe Barbera said it was the most sophisticated cartoon they had ever tried.

"When you did a cartoon for H-B, first you sent them a tape, then you came in for an audition. Now, they had three actors under contract: Lenny Weinrib, Daws Butler, and Don Messick, three legendary voice actors. They did most of the voices. You only got hired if none of the three could imitate your voice. And none of them could do mine!

"This was a gang show. Like *McHale's Navy*. An ensemble. They had to get voices that were very distinctive, yet blended together. We all worked great together.

"And we did 'em fast. I don't recall any session going over an hour and a half.

"Most of us were old radio actors, and they're the best.

"Choo Choo, the part I played, was the cat that went to CCNY. He was the intellect of the group. He always wore a turtleneck and he loved Top Cat. He would never question any of Top Cat's ideas, although he never thought any of Top Cat's ideas were very great. Choo Choo would intellectualize everything. He was the intellectual of the group.

"All the characters were harmless. Not like the characters in cartoons today. They were very kind to each other and liked each other."

The geniuses behind *Top Cat* were, of course, Joe Barbera and Bill Hannah.

Bill was a rather quiet man, he was kind and creative, but Joe was always center-stage and flamboyant. The extrovert and the introvert.

Joe was magic. He was razzle-dazzle. He was mercury. He was a magnificent, kind human being. He was a doer. Always active.

"Working for H-B was the best of times. Very happy experiences. Animation and cartoons were a very high level. The shows were intellectual. There was some content to them. Characters were kind and generous and warm and humanistic and philanthropic.

"We're living in different times now.

"I would describe *Top Cat* as top quality in the writing, in concept, and in the performances. Beautiful."

The voices of Top Cat. *From left to right bottom row: Allen Jenkins, Arnold Stang, and Maurice Gosfield. From left to right top row: Leo DeLyon, Marvin, and John Stephenson. (1961-1962).*

Marvin the School Teacher

While a student at Brooklyn College, Marvin got a part-time job teaching across the street from the college at Midwood High School. "To become a permanent teacher, I had to take a speech test. I flunked. So I stayed on as a substitute."

And teaching became his second love. When he moved to Hollywood there was a lot of down time for anyone who wanted to act for a living. Some actors spent their days and nights in the bleachers at Dodger Stadium, some headed for the golf course or the tennis courts, some frequented their favorite watering hole, but Marvin chose to continue on as a substitute teacher.

Away from acting, Marvin taught over 3,000 high school classes in the Los Angeles public school system.

I had called Marvin three days in a row, leaving a message each time. He finally called me back.

"Where were you?" I asked, thinking he was out of town on location somewhere.

"Teaching," he answered.

"Teaching?" I was surprised. I didn't know.

"Biology," he said. "What a joke," he continued. "I was the only one in my bio class who flunked!" Then I heard that laugh of his, a combination of a foghorn and a donkey's bray.

"Sorry I didn't get back to you sooner, but those kids wear me out and at night I just don't feel like talking anymore."

I understood. But now he was ready to talk.

"Ask me why I teach."

"Okay, Marvin, why do you teach?"

"It's gonna sound schmaltzy."

"Try me."

"Because I think it's being a good citizen. I feel like I'm contributing. Schmaltzy, no?"

"Yes, Marvin, very schmaltzy."

"Look," he says, "Some actors get involved with politics, some do benefits. I teach. Otherwise, what would I do with my spare time? Hang around the house? Wait for my agent to call? This way I keep busy, and the kids are a great audience!"

"Do you ever try out new material on them?" I asked, trying to be funny.

"All the time. I tell them stories I've written and sing songs that I've composed. They applaud, they laugh. They're my best audience!"

"I don't know if they're your best audience but they're certainly a captive audience. Do they know you're a famous actor?"

"If they don't, I tell 'em! Inevitably, on the first day in class someone will say, "Aren't you in the movies? And I tell them people are always getting me mixed up with Rock Hudson!"

Whether they knew Marvin or not, besides entertaining them, he was teaching them and motivating them.

He told me once that every teacher in America should be handed an Oscar every single day for their performances to teach and keep their students attentive.

"It's a tough, strength-sapping job," he told me.

Marvin didn't just teach in the exclusive high rent places like Brentwood and Westwood. He also taught in tough, slum-like neighborhoods in Compton and East LA.

"What would you do if you got a bad kid looking for trouble? What if he tried to give you a hard time?"

"No different than a heckler in a night club, I guess," Marvin thought. "You try to calm him down with humor. If I can say something funny, make the class laugh, but not at the bad kid's expense, I can usually win them over. But to be honest with you, over 3,000 classes, and I've never had a problem.

Of course he had never had a problem. From school kids to senior citizens, they all loved Marvin.

On the set of The Fabulous Señorita *starring Estelita Rodriguez as herself and featuring a young Marvin. (1952)*

Who Did You Hate?

The problem with Marvin was he loved people. He adored actors. Whenever I would ask him about someone he worked with, it was always, "I loved him. He was a wonderful person. A great actor. A sweet person. Very talented." And on and on.

So one day I asked him over a bowl of matzo ball chicken soup, "Who did you hate? There must have been some actor or actress who you did not like. Yes?"

Marvin thought between spoonfuls.

Finally, he said, "Jerry Lewis. Not a nice man. When we did *The Nutty Professor* no one told me he was addicted to percodan. He was very sick but I didn't know.

"We would rehearse, but it didn't make a lot of sense because we improvised everything. And then, if you improvised over and over you lost the spontaneity of the moment, which is what he was going for.

"One day he tried to run me over with a kiddy car. He thought it was funny. I didn't. "Instead of apologizing, he tells me I'm too lovable, that audiences would hate him if he made fun of me or was mean to me. He said, 'Working with you, Marvin, is like working with Shirley Booth.'

"All of a sudden he's comparing me to Shirley Booth, a great, great actress. It made no sense.

"Then there was the day I'm in makeup early in the morning, and Jerry walks in with a gun. A gun! And he shoots the darn thing! I fell out of the makeup chair probably thinking he was shooting at me. He laughed. I didn't.

"Later I went up to him and told him that I'd have to quit the picture because I was 4-F, and maybe all this physical activity was too much for me. He left me alone after that.

"I only had one or two lines in the picture, and the way Jerry shot my scene I knew it was going to end up on the cutting room floor. And it did. He cut me out of the picture and made me look like an extra.

"Now, here's the funny part. Actually, not so funny.

"He hires me to make personal appearances for the movie! I'm going around the country publicizing the film, telling my audiences what a great director Jerry is, and what a wonderful person he is, and how funny he is, and I'm lying on the cutting room floor, completely out of the picture!

"Wait," says Marvin, salting what's left of his matzo ball, "there's more. He invites me to come up to Vegas to be a guest on his yearly telethon. He wants me to play Henry, the telephone repair man, that I was playing at that time on *Alice*.

"I go up to Vegas, put on my Henry outfit, and Jerry never introduces me, never acknowledges me, but sticks me in the middle of the phone banks to take pledges from the people calling in. I knew it was for a good cause, but I'm a regular on a hit series, at least introduce me!

"Later, when we all went back to the dressing room we found all our clothes scattered all over the floor. There had been a bomb scare but Jerry never told anyone, which I thought was really shitty of him.

"And, guess what? There was a bomb. It had been planted on his plane! We never found out if the bomb was loaded or not, but either way that's pretty scary stuff.

"Jerry surrounded himself with 'yes' people. People who were afraid to disagree with him.

"I think he wanted me to be one of his 'yes' people. He asked for my phone number one day on the set. I refused to give it to him. All the cast used to say he would call them at two o'clock in the morning. I didn't need that.

"He was a very lonely man. Very lonely."

"Who else didn't you like?" I asked as we ordered a piece of strudel to share.

"I was once sitting with Joanne Woodward and Thelma Ritter in the Paramount commissary. I forget what was said, but the three of us starting laughing hysterically and couldn't stop. John Wayne must have thought we were laughing at him, and he literally threw us out of the commissary. We left laughing all the way!

"He was a big star. Maybe the biggest. And if he didn't like somebody, they better not be in his world! As an arch conservative, you better agree with his politics or else.

"Joanne, Thelma, and I were not of the same persuasion. Maybe that's why he kicked us out. I don't really know."

I was wiping the strudel crumbs off my shirt. "Anybody else?"

"Shelly Winters was very temperamental. When she was good she was a lot of fun to be with, but if things weren't going her way she could be bitchy. She was not easy to work with."

"Anybody else?"

"That's it," he said as he started to hunt through his wallet with his bad eyesight to split the bill with me.

"That's okay, Marvin, I got it."

I would pay ten times as much just to listen to Marvin's stories.

On the set of the TV series, Meet Millie, *from left to right: Florence Halop, Marvin, and Elena Verdugo (1952-1955).*

Meet Millie

"A gay, new comedy about the life and loves of a secretary in Manhattan. It's time to meet Millie."

And so, for 78 episodes on CBS, audiences tuned in first on radio, then on television, to meet Millie Bronson from 1951 to 1955.

Marvin played the aspiring poet and friend, the geeky and eccentric Alfred Prinzmetal, who dropped in every week for a neighborly visit. His visits always provided laughs and sage advice from Millie.

Marvin had a recurring line that he recited on every show. The audience would wait for it and it always caused great laughter. Looking at Millie and her mother, with eyes that drooped behind those thick, round, black-framed glasses and a Brooklynese mournful, heartbreaking voice, Marvin would lament, "You people hate me!" The audience would howl.

One columnist wrote, "You can't help breaking up. He's so sad it's a scream!"

And Marvin had the last word. "I love to laugh. Someone once said my laugh is like a donkey *praying*. I said I didn't even know they went to church!

"I laugh for free, but I get paid to look sad and miserable."

Meet Millie was one of the first live shows with a live audience. Unlike today, when the audience would burst out laughing at a funny sequence, the actors would literally freeze in position until the laughter stopped.

Marvin said, "It was like doing a Broadway play every week. If somebody went up on their lines there was no stopping, no reshooting. We plowed ahead, sometimes rewriting as we went along until we could slip back into the script.

"The worst part," recollected Marvin, "was that all the episodes were destroyed. No reruns, no residuals. I heard there might be one or two episodes that were saved, that some collector has them. But I've never seen them."

Another time, when Marvin and I were sitting in my living room waiting for my writer's workshop to begin, he made an interesting comment about *Meet Millie*. "See if this sounds familiar," he said. "Millie, played by Elena Verdugo, a single woman in her mid-twenties, divides her time between her job and her home life, going on dates, living in a Manhattan brownstone, and putting up with a cranky boss." Marvin decided *Meet Millie* was the forerunner for *The Mary Tyler Moore Show*.

Marvin loved the early days of television because the shows were shown live. No tape delay, no do-overs. "We worked over 60 hours a week," Marvin was telling my writer's workshop. "Every week for over two years with no days off! Little time for rehearsals, so when a prop didn't work, or a set fell down, or the kid holding cue cards screwed up, we somehow carried on. Live television was like opening in New Haven, but there was no New Haven.

"Costume changes were made on the run so you could be ready for your next entrance. Some actors wore two or three costumes at once. They would strip them off layer by layer for their different scenes. And when the shows were done, the tapes were destroyed.

Nobody thought of saving shows in those days. Except Desilu. They were smarter than everybody else.

Marvin and Erena Verdugo, who played Millie, became life-long friends. "We all bonded on the show. We were like family because we never got to see our own families. You can't go through the torture we went through without getting collectively and psychologically burnt-out. Elena and I have twin scars that we shared for the rest of our lives."

Marvin's character, Alfred E. Prinzmetal, the failed poet, was the shy, introverted, timid, nervous, "nebbish," loser geek. And America loved him. He was them, they were him.

He played that same type character over and over, and audiences would welcome his appearance on stage, in films, or on TV.

They all knew the face, the glasses, the voice. But only the most rapid fans knew his name.

1951. Marvin was offered two radio shows and had to choose. He chose The Three of Us over the other new show *Meet Millie*. To play the part of Millie they wanted Judy Holiday, but Marvin thought that he and Holiday's humor was too similar, their characters too much alike, so Marvin chose *The Three of Us*.

How many actors would have given their right arm to have a similar dilemma?

The producer of both radio shows was Cy Howard, probably the biggest name in radio comedies. But Marvin called him a "gonif," a Yiddish word for thief.

"He stole everything," Marvin told me over the phone one day. "He stole my friend Irma from a show called *My Sister Eileen*. And he stole *Life of Luigi* from *The Education of Hyman Kaplan*. Hyman Kaplan was Jewish, Luigi was Italian, otherwise exactly the same. And Eileen and Irma could have been twins!

"A wonderful actor named Ed Max recommended me to Cy. Cy had just been arrested, caught in a house of prostitution, and was on parole. One day, Cy told the cast not to be upset if policemen came to visit him in the booth."

Marvin had never done radio before. He thought his job was to memorize the script. When they started to rehearse and the cast of Eddie Max, Sandra Gould, and Hans Conreid began reading off the pages, they were startled to see Marvin knew by heart his lines, and everybody else's! Cy Howard couldn't believe what he had just seen—an actor memorizing a radio script!

CBS decided not to pick up the show even though Marvin thought the pilot was very funny, with the audience howling with laughter. Maybe the network figured having a producer who was picked up and arrested in a whorehouse was not an ideal image for CBS.

But then they did go for *Meet Millie*. Go figure.

And since Marvin had turned down *Meet Millie*, they had hired an actor named Bill Tracy.

For whatever reason, Bill Tracy wasn't working out, so Cy Howard wrote Marvin into one of the scripts. And thus was born Alfred E. Printzmetal, and that distinctive, plaintive Brooklynese voice and character won over the radio audiences.

CBS was flooded with thousands of letters asking what was the name of the actor playing Alfred E. Printzmetal?

Well it didn't take long. Bill Tracy was out, Marvin was in.

✖ ✖ ✖

Marvin drove the same old, dirty car for years. He once joked, "I get my car washed once a year whether it needs it or not."

He and Elena Vurdugo were going to a fancy Hollywood premier together. Marvin picked Elena up in his junky, dirty jalopy. They pulled up in front of the theater, and with hundreds of fans waiting anxiously to see what celebrities were arriving, Marvin opened the door for Elena and the door fell off, clanging on the red carpet!

And Marvin wasn't kidding about the once-a-year car wash. The first time he took his junk-on-wheels to be washed, the attendant told him to close the windows, put the car in neutral, and release the brake. Same thing he would tell every customer. What he didn't tell Marvin was to get out of the car! Before Marvin knew it, the car lurched forward and Marvin watched from the inside of his car, being sprayed, soaped, and splashed.

Arriving at the end of the ride, Marvin sheepishly got out to the applause from those patrons waiting for their cars. He turned to his audience and said, "They told me to close the windows, put it in neutral, and release the brake. But," he shrugs, "nobody told me to get out!"

It is believed this is a photo of Rosa Felsenburg, Marvin's wife. (c1973)

Rosa & Shirley

On June 3rd, 1973, at the Statler Hilton Hotel on 7th Avenue and 33rd Street in Manhattan, Marvin Kaplan married Rosa Felsenburg.

Marvin was 46, Rosa, 47.

It was an orthodox wedding ending with Marvin, under the "huppah" (a canopy of flowers), stomping on and smashing a wineglass. The rabbi reminded the couple that marriages are as fragile as glass and must always be treated with care, love, and respect.

Three years later they were divorced. They did not have children.

"We were both set in our way," Marvin said at Mort's Deli between bites of his corned beef sandwich. "It was not a good marriage."

They had met in high school. Life took them on separate paths. He ended up in Hollywood, she became a college professor in Indianapolis, Indiana.

Many years later, Marvin and Rosa ran into each other on a street in Indianapolis. A long way from Brooklyn. They decided to keep in touch. Not many months later they decided to marry. The wedding was in New York, but they immediately moved into Marvin's modest two-bedroom house in Burbank.

On its cleanest days, the house was a pigsty. Marvin was not the neatest guy, and he was a hoarder. Not a good combination for Rosa, who was organized and meticulously neat.

"My house always looked like it had just been robbed," he would say. He loved to tell this story: "Right after the big earthquake we had here in '71, a neighbor knocked on my door to check on my damage. In truth, I was lucky. There was absolutely no damage to the house. But the neighbor took one look at the mess inside and told me that with so much destruction they'd probably have to bulldoze the place and start all over!

"In truth, I had the same cleaning lady for over thirty years. Because for a number of years she was in a wheel chair she couldn't do such a good job of cleaning. But she was with me for thirty years! Who could fire her? So maybe she couldn't reach a few spots to clean. Nobody cared. Until Rosa moved in."

Rosa wasn't happy. "She expected me to be the same person she knew from Brooklyn. I expected her to have changed. Both of us were wrong."

While Marvin was busy doing mostly guest spots on TV, Rosa became the first full-time woman faculty member at Hebrew Union College in Los Angeles.

It appears Rosa struggled with the role of a woman in contemporary Jewish life. On one hand, she was teaching the old Talmudic traditions of being a good Orthodox Jewish wife, a helpmate to the husband, and running a kosher household.

On the other hand (as Tevya would say), she was a strong advocate for feminism, fighting for women's rights, equal pay in the workplace, and equality in the home.

Rosa was also a published poet. Two of her long poems appear in *Blood to Remember: American Poets on the Holocaust* and *Sarah's Daughters Sing: A Sampler of Poems by Jewish Women*.

She also wrote essays, such as "The Noah Syndrome," which was published originally in the book *On Being a Jewish Feminist*.

Neither Marvin or Rosa remarried.

Rosa passed away at 86 in 2011.

Even before he married Rosa, Marvin had a dear friend, an actress named Shirley Cytron. They met at Stage Society, where they worked on scenes together and even acted in plays together.

As a teenager, she had started out with Ronald Reagan and others on Warner Brothers radio in such shows as *American Marches On*, which were dramatic reenactments of historical happenings. She later worked on TV, had some small parts in a few movies, and continued working in theater.

And even as Marvin's fame grew, he and Shirley never lost touch. Always good friends.

At one point, Marvin proposed to Shirley.

"Shirley, how long have we known each other?"

Shirley smiled. "Longer than either of us can remember."

Marvin with Shirley Cytron. (c2016)

Marvin wiped his glasses with his shirt. "Maybe we should get married."

Shirley was taken by surprise. "Who?"

Marvin, in that Brooklynese, "What do you mean, 'who'? Us. You and me. What, we haven't known each other long enough?"

Shirley sighed. "Marvin, I've done that already. Twice. I don't want to do that anymore."

"Don't you think we'd be good together?"

"We'd be terrific together."

"So?"

"Listen to me, your eyesight is not so good. Your hearing is going. You have a hard time walking. Marvin, you don't need a wife you need a caretaker. And that's one audition I'm not going on!"

So they remained good friends for the rest of their lives.

He would take her to the Academy Awards ceremonies. They'd walk down the red carpet holding hands like two middle-aged lovers.

She would stand patiently by when Marvin would stop to do a TV interview. And though I don't personally know this, I'll bet Marvin never did an interview where he didn't introduce Shirley.

And Marvin became part of Shirley's family. Thanksgiving, his birthday, her birthday, Marvin was always invited. In fact, at the Passover "Seders," Marvin was the one who recited the prayers in Hebrew.

When they weren't together, they'd talk on the phone.

And gifts. Marvin took such delight in buying gifts for friends. And all thoughtful stuff. My wife, Connie, got some wonderful presents through the years. And so did I.

And so did Shirley. Jewelry, a watch, scarves, blouses, sweaters.

One of Shirley's favorite "gifts" was when Marvin was casting *Look Out for Slick*, a feature film he wrote in my workshop. He was giving out parts to all his friends, but he really didn't have a part for Shirley. But because he wanted her to be in the film, his "gift" to Shirley was to cast her as "a person who is sleeping on the grass."

So through long rehearsals, Shirley, with no dialogue and no action, played on the grass. She may have actually fallen asleep. Who would know!

And when Marvin would tell that story around the Passover table, he'd burst out into his hee-haw-signature laugh.

On August 25, 2016, Marvin was supposed to be at Shirley's 96th birthday.

But that was the day he died.

.

On the set of Alice with Marvin as Henry, Vic Tayback as Mel, and
Beth Holland as Vera. (1976-1985)

ALICE

In 1975, there was a successful movie called *Alice Doesn't Live Here Anymore*. It starred Ellen Burnstyn and was the story of a widow and her 12-year-old son who leave their home in New Jersey and head for Hollywood so she can pursue her dream of becoming a professional singer.

But when her car breaks down outside of Phoenix, she is forced to take a job as a waitress at a roadside diner.

CBS decided that movie would make a great sitcom. And so, shortening the title and hiring Linda Lavin to play the title character, Alice stayed in Arizona and Mel's Diner for nine years and 202 episodes as one of television's most beloved shows, *Alice*.

In early 1976, Marvin's agent, Meyer Mishkin, called Marvin and told him Warner Bros. wanted him for a new TV series based on the movie *Alice Doesn't Live Here Anymore*. They were actually offering Marvin two different parts, and they were sending scripts over to him so he could decide which character he wanted to play.

One of the parts was a telephone repair man, the other was the father of the teenage boy.

Marvin read the scripts, called Mishkin, and together they thought the repairman offered more possibilities.

So Marvin became Henry Beesmeyer, a regular customer at the diner.

Marvin and I were on the phone a couple of years ago. He was concerned about how to introduce a new character in the script he was writing and keep the story flowing.

Somehow the conversation got around to *Alice*. "Here's how I was introduced to the audience. I'm sitting at the counter when the phone keeps ringing. So my character, Henry, says, 'Please answer the phone. It's making me very nervous. Please, somebody, answer the phone!'

Marvin as Henry the telephone repairman/poet in Alice. (1978-1985)

"I'm getting agitated, which I can play real good. When no one in the diner answered the phone, I leapt off my seat mumbling, 'That's it!' and I ripped the phone off the wall and carried it outside. My line was 'I'm from the phone company and you folks need a new one anyway!'

"The audience loved it! The show was an instant success and so was I!

"Now they had to keep me around because I was the only one who could fix the phone!"

Marvin became a regular on the show from then on.

A running gag was that Henry was always making jokes about Mel's cooking. He'd threaten to take his business over to Barney's Burger Barn or Vinnie's House of Veal, Mel's Diner's two biggest competitors. But, of course, he never did.

Later in the series, Henry's wife, Chloe, played by Ruth Ruzzi, was introduced. However, she only appeared in one episode. But Henry talked about her all the time. In fact, the main reason Henry hung out at the diner was to get away from Chloe. Evidently, they didn't have the best relationship.

Henry once said, "I'd like Chloe to be a den mother—with real lions."

Marvin, as Henry, stayed with the show until it closed in 1985.

Sometimes, Henry was the butt of the joke. Like, for instance, this exchange between Mel and one of the waitresses, Vera. Henry wasn't in this scene, but the dialogue was too precious, and it's one of my favorite scenes!

Vera brings Mel some chicken that was a cooked in the diner:
Mel: It's so salty!
Vera: Oh, we got salt in everything.
Mel: Why?
Vera: We used the salt to put out the fire.
Mel: What fire?
Vera: The fire that started from the grease.
Mel: What grease?
*Vera: The grease from when we cooked 20 pounds of bacon
    and 13 pork chops!*

Mel: When did you cook 20 pounds of bacon and 13 pork
   chops?
Vera: We had to before they spoiled.
Mel: Why would they spoil?
Vera: Oh, well, someone left the freezer door open all night
   during the excitement when the paramedics came.
Mel: Paramedics!
Vera: Yes! They had to take some stitches in Henry's head.
Mel: Stitches in Henry's head?!
Vera: Yes! I dropped a pie on the floor and he slipped in
   it and hit his head on the counter. And that's why your
   chicken is salty!

Marvin was hired for a part in one episode and had only three lines. "I think," Marvin told me, "I milked those three lines pretty good, because we got a lot of laughs. Of course they were from the laugh-machine, but they were funny lines. I had fun doing the part. Linda Lavin and Vic Tayback and the rest of the company liked what I did, and so did the studio audience. So, next thing I know, they had me come back, then a third time, and before I knew it, Henry, the phone repair man, became a regular on the show!"

I asked him if he remembered the episode where someone threw a bowl of spaghetti in his face. To which he says, "I was working! Spaghetti, meat balls, tomato sauce, whatever! As long as I had the job!"

Even now, after all these years, somewhere in the world, Mel's Diner is still open for business.

THE FIVE PHASES OF AN ACTOR'S LIFE

In the beginning, a producer asks, "Who is Marvin Kaplan?" Nobody knows him, nobody wants to take a chance on him, nobody hires him.

Then, miracle of miracles, he gets the job acting in *Adam's Rib*. He now graduates to a second plateau. Studio Executives are now saying, "Let's get Marvin Kaplan."

Now he starts working regularly. Movie parts, guest appearances on TV shows, he becomes a regular on a series; he's starting to make good money. Now producers think they'd like to hire Marvin, but he's too expensive, so they say, "Get me a Marvin Kaplan-type!"

And finally, the last plateau. Marvin's eye sight is not good, his hearing is not good, he's confined to a wheelchair, phone calls are not returned, and producers ask, "Who is this guy who keeps calling. Anybody know a Marvin Kaplan?

Chicago Teddy Bears

CBS thought they had a winner in 1971 in a TV series called *Chicago Teddy Bears*. The show was supposed to be a satire on *The Untouchables*, a successful series about FBI agent Elliot Ness, a true-life character, and his unrelentless search and capture of gangland's biggest criminals.

Marvin played the mob's bookkeeper on *Teddy Bears*. "I was supposed to be the accountant, a good, decent man working for guys whose business was murder, racketeering, robberies, and more murder. I was supposed to be scared to death of my so-called employers.

"The only problem was the gangsters and the killers came across as pussycats! No one ever got murdered, maimed, beaten-up, or scratched.

"Instead of doing a take-off on *The Untouchables*, we were doing a gang comedy like *Hogan's Heroes* or *McHale's Navy*. You couldn't tell the good guys from the bad guys.

"Baby Face Nelson was concerned with going on a diet, Two Gun McGinty wanted to design woman's fashions, Al Capone was always sucking lollypops. Their guns were made of Hershey's chocolate, and they'd try to drown their victims in mounds of whipped cream!

"And for what I had to do on the show, they might as well have written me out. Each week my part got smaller and more insignificant."

The show was short-lived. Instead of satire, the writers delivered silly. The ratings shriveled as the audience began seeking other channels.

One of Marvin's closest friends on the show was 6 feet 5 inches tall, gruff, tough-looking Mike Mazurki. Mike always played a thug, a gangster, or a hitman.

"He was one of the gentlest people I ever met," Marvin told me as we sat in my car one day waiting for the rain to stop. "That was the problem with the show, all the villains were sweet, kind people. Mike was a wonderful actor, and I was shocked and disappointed when I came on the set one day and was told Mike had been fired.

"Why him?! He was a sweet man, and though all the gangsters were interchangeable, why make him the scapegoat?

"Believe me, if they were going to fire anyone, it should have been me! Talk about an insignificant character!

"I'll say this for the producers of the show, they didn't know what the hell they were doing!"

The series was supposed to be a comeback project for Ann Southern. She played a street flower vendor in the pilot, but then was written out when the series went on the air.

After three months, CBS cancelled the show and Marvin was momentarily out of work.

On the Air

The shortest TV series Marvin was featured in was a sitcom titled *On the Air*, and it ran for 3 episodes in the States in 1992 on ABC.

Seven episodes were filmed, and all seven ran in England and across Europe.

The story was about a fictional television network in the 1950's, producing a live variety show called *The Lester Guy Show*.

The show-inside-the-show was a disaster. But then, so was the show-outside-the-show.

Marvin played Dwight McGonigle, the producer of *The Lester Guy Show*. Lester Guy was played by Ian Buchanan.

McGonigle suffered from hay-fever. Given an antihistamine, it would transfer his personality into Snaps, a dog who was the 'Spokesdog' for Snaps brand dog food, *The Lester Guy Show*'s sponsor.

Only water could break the spell.

One other thing about McGonigle, he was not from this planet! When *The Lester Guy Show* would get out of control, McGonigle would revert back to his former life on a planet somewhere in a distant dimension. That's when Marvin would recite the line, "From so far away she calls to me".

The show came from the mind of way-out director David Lynch. That it lasted three shows was surely a David Lynch miracle.

Wild at Heart

In 1990, Marvin played Uncle Pooch in David Lynch's crime drama *Wild at Heart*. The movie, starring Nicholas Cage and Laura Dern, is filled with scenes of mutilation, derangement, corruption, and killings. Not exactly the kind of romantic comedies Marvin had been featured in.

Marvin loved working with Lynch. Marvin called Lynch the Orson Wells of his generation, a genius film maker. He was very meticulous. Even though Lynch wanted Marvin to improvise his scene with Laura Dern, Lynch would describe the kind of background music he would use, the camera placement and lenses he would employ, the kind of lighting he would use, and as Marvin said, "50 different details" before he would shoot the scene.

Marvin later worked with Lynch on the short-lived TV series *On the Air*. The series that lasted 3 weeks in the States, though 7 episodes were shot.

Marvin claimed that of all the directors he worked with, Lynch was the master. His understanding of film-making far surpassed all the other directors Marvin had worked for.

The problem with David Lynch? He'd get bored. He'd walk away from a project right in the middle of the series because he would lose interest in the project, according to Marvin.

He would assign other people to direct, people not nearly as talented or lacking Lynch's insight. The actors, including Marvin, were perplexed as to where to go with their characters or where the story was headed because Lynch wasn't around to offer direction or advice.

Lynch's movies and TV series are complex and somewhat bewildering. So is the man.

BECKER

Becker was a sitcom starring Ted Danson as a grumpy neighborhood doctor always gruff, always annoyed, never a winner, but loved by his patients and friends despite his foibles. The show ran from 1998 to 2004.

Marvin played Mr. Gordon and guest starred in a few episodes.

In an episode titled "Man Plans God Laughs," Becker is hounded by one of his patients, a tiny, tiny over 80 year old lady who wants Becker to prepare her for her death even though he keeps insisting she is very healthy and has nothing wrong with her.

When she brings into the office a number of different outfits to ask Becker what she should wear in the coffin, he loses his patience.

As a last resort, he grabs another patient, Mr. Gordon, played by Marvin, and insisted Mr. Gordon help the old lady pick out the right dress to be buried in. As Mr. Gordon and the old lady leave the office, Marvin turns to Ted Danson, and as only Marvin could say it, with a twinkle in his eye, proclaims, "She's a hottie! I don't know how to thank you." To which Becker, shoving Marvin out of the office, responds, "Just seeing the two of you leave is thanks enough," as he closes the door on Mr. Gordon.

In an episode in season three titled "Trials and Defibulations," Mr. Gordon (Marvin) has gone on a starvation diet to look slim enough to wear his good suit for a wedding he's going to be attending.

When he gets dizzy and feels faint, he tracks Becker down in a courtroom where he's falsely being sued for malpractice. Becker holds up the hearing to listen to Marvin's symptoms, tells him his blood sugar's too low, gets him some candy, and Marvin feels better.

Also in season one, there was an episode titled "Truth and Consequences," where Mr. Gordon goes to see Becker because he's got a new girlfriend and he wants to be checked for AIDS!

In Becker's office, the conversation goes like this:

BECKER
What's new, Mr. Gordon?

GORDON
I want an AIDS test.

BECKER
Let's go back to "What's new?"

GORDON
You see, Doctor, I started dating a
younger woman. She's 65.

BECKER
Her parents are okay with that? Let me
ask you something. When's the last time
you had sex?

GORDON
1986.

BECKER
That's what we in the medical profession
call a very long time. You don't need this test.

GORDON
I read all those articles in newspapers.
I want to be safe and responsible.

BECKER
If you were any safer you'd be in different
cities! Alright, alright, if you insist I'm going
to have to draw some blood and ask you some
questions. Have you ever had any transfusions?
Any drug use? Homosexual activity?

GORDON
No.
(beat)
And I think I'd remember!
(beat)
Although, I did black out for a few hours
on VJ Day.

Later in the episode, Becker tells Mr. Gordon the HIV test came back negative. Mr. Gordon tells Becker he hasn't had sex since his wife died, and he reads in all the magazines about how times have changed and there are new ways to make love and, obviously, he wants to make his new girlfriend happy.

Becker reassures Mr. Gordon that the most important thing about sex is that both people must enjoy themselves.

GORDON
Both people?
(he thinks)
Times have changed!

It would be the last series in which Marvin would have a reoccurring role.

On the set of A New Kind of Love *with from left to right: Ralph Harold, Marvin, Paul Newman, and George Tobias. (1963)*

ON WRITING

Marvin never wanted to be a professional actor. What he always wanted to be was a writer.

He started writing plays at summer camp when he was 10 or 11.

In high school, he had a play he wrote and performed in college. "My play was accepted at Yale, but I wasn't. One of the characters in the play was based on me, but they told me I was wrong for the part!

"In those days actors were either 'pretty boys' or tall, handsome men. I wasn't tall enough."

In Hollywood, between jobs, Marvin worked as a substitute teacher. Although, one time he actually got into Warner Brothers as a bookkeeper. "I was the worst bookkeeper they ever saw. Every minute I wasn't adding or subtracting, I was writing scripts."

Eventually he sold scripts to radio dramas or TV anthology shows.

For the California Artists Radio Theater, he wrote the script and the lyrics for *A Good House for a Killing*, their most successful musical-comedy.

The story is also a perfect example of Marvin's type of humor.

In *A Good House for a Killing*, an adult son decides to kill off his parents for the inheritance. He hires a killer to do the job. On Passover, the entire family is around the dinner table reading about the struggle between Moses and the Pharaoh.

At one point in the ceremony, the angel Elijah comes into the home and drinks from a special cup of wine set in the center of the table. Every kid waits for that magic moment. And every kid is convinced that Elijah sips from that cup because every kid can see the wine getting lower in the glass.

And, to welcome Elijah, the youngest kid runs to the front door, opens it, and welcomes the angel into the home.

Only in Marvin's play it's not Elijah that comes in, it's the killer.

But the kid thinks he's the angel and invites him to stay for Passover dinner!

That's Marvin's sense of humor!

Marvin not only wrote for the theater, he wrote for television as well. He wrote episodes for *The Adams Family*, *The Bill Cosby Show*, *Mod Squad*, and *Maude*.

He wrote plays for Theater West, one of the oldest and most prestigious theater companies in Los Angeles.

And, of course, in the last years of his life, along with his friend Steve Carter, he wrote and produced *Watch Out for Slick* and *Looking Up*.

MARVIN KAPLAN

Unions

Every family has at least one rich uncle. And Marvin had his. He owned one of the largest pickle factories in all of New York state.

Marvin, probably when he was in college, worked at the pickle factory one summer.

The workers in the plant were unhappy. Wages were low, conditions were poor, hours were long. Marvin organized the workers. He led them in walking off their jobs.

And who was at the forefront of the picketers? Marvin, champion of worker's rights, spokesman of the unwashed!

And who was Marvin striking? His uncle! The workers' demands were met and Marvin went back to college.

Marvin's first involvement with a union began years later in 1954. Associates of his, top radio actors, were being accused of being communists.

"The McCarthy thing was terrible. Nobody knew what the hell was going on except that this guy McCarthy was on some kind of a witch hunt.

"It was in our union's constitution in AFTRA (American Federation of Television and Radio Artists)—local and national—that no one could remain a member of AFTRA who was ever a member of the Communist Party, had ever give his money or talent to the Party, or was ever a member of any organization found by due process of law to be subversive. People signed loyalty oaths.

"I was teaching at the time at a high school as a substitute teacher. I had to sign a loyalty oath. On it was a list of things considered communistic, and one was Brooklyn College. I told them I couldn't sign their loyalty oath. I went to Brooklyn College. Over five thousand people went to Brooklyn College! You think they were all communists?

"On the list was the Boy Scouts. Ridiculous. Actors' careers were cut short because of the blacklist. And because of that they didn't have enough years in the union to qualify for the Motion Picture Home. You had to have so many years working in the industry to qualify for the benefits of retiring to live at the Home. It was a terrible time."

✖ ✖ ✖

Is it any wonder that when aging actors were seeking an advocate to be their voice with their union that Marvin was the chosen one?

Marvin spoke at an AFTRA Los Angeles, local meeting.

"These are not good times for older actors and actresses. All your many years, all your experience learning your craft, wasted by Hollywood's fascination for young, handsome, and beautiful.

"They portray us two steps from humility and five steps from the grave.

"It's a vicious slander and we don't deserve it!"

Marvin won the election and became president of The LA Chapter of AFTRA.

He served two separate terms, 1989-1995 and 2003-2005.

He also served on the board of Screen Actors Guild, 1975-84, including a two-year term as vice president.

He was also involved with Actors' Equity, California Artists Radio Theater, and Theatre West.

In other words, Marvin was a joiner. Better than that, he was an activist who spoke out and got involved.

He promoted and encouraged senior actors. He was painfully aware of a real ageism prejudice against senior performers.

More than once he told me how much he loved older actors. I overheard him talking to one of the writers in my workshop.

"I still am in awe of good older actors and actresses. They come prepared. They know their lines. They're always "up," always enthusiastic, and always with lots of energy.

"But older actors are having a rough time getting jobs these days, me included, because the business is youth orientated.

"All that good talent being wasted."

Later, Marvin would personally do something about it.

AND HERE'S WHAT HIS FRIENDS REMEMBER...

Steven Carter was Marvin's co-writer.
Bumpy Roads
Back in the day, when Marvin still drove, but before his eye surgery, he would often come to our house for dinner. Marvin loved home-cooked meals! We lived in a corner house, two blocks off of Buena Vista Street along Chandler Blvd in Burbank.

There's a North Chandler and a South Chandler separated—back then—by railroad tracks. It's a walk/bike track now. I used to wait in the yard with my two kids when I knew Marvin was coming over. It was to keep him from missing the house and driving right by.

Marvin saw the street sign to our street, turned on his signal and turned left—right onto the railroad tracks. From the yard, we watched as Marvin continued down the tracks for the two blocks to our house. He was bouncing around like an echo in a canyon.

My kids ran to the fence calling Marvin's name. He heard them, then saw them and, without missing a beat, Marvin turned off of the tracks, drove through the bushes, down the curb, and parked...facing the wrong way. As he got out of the car all he said in his famous deadpan voice was, "I don't remember that road being that rough."

Driver's License Renewal
This story occurred before Marvin had his eye surgery. His driver's license was about to expire. We discussed that maybe it was time to stop driving and to hire a driver.

Marvin, being Marvin, wanted to renew his license. He was stubborn that way. He went to the DMV, and the woman helping him was a huge fan. She was a bit loud, jovial, and very animated with a heavy southern accent.

Marvin played it up and had this woman laughing so hard that she was crying. There are three different eye charts mounted a specified distance from the counter. The clerk asked Marvin to read from the middle eye chart. Marvin looked in the direction the clerk was pointing and simply asked, "There's an eye chart up there?" The woman laughed and said, "You are so funny. There are three. Read from the middle one." Marvin started calling out random letters, making the woman laugh even harder. It didn't help that Marvin was laughing too.

Finally, the clerk asked Marvin to read from one of the other two charts. Marvin, with total sincerity asked, "There are really three charts up there?" The woman laughed until she ached.

Marvin's moment of glory came when he slammed down his renewed driver's license, admitting to me that he never saw a single letter. The woman thought he was kidding, playing a role. Marvin, thanks to his good sense, stopped driving shortly after his license was renewed. Only Marvin could have gotten away with a feat like that!

Marvin's Love of Life

Marvin cherished every single day of his life. He loved life. He used to say to me, "We'll be dead a whole lot longer than we'll be alive, so I want every second." He said, "If I'm ever in a coma and the doctors say that I only have one chance in a million of surviving, I want that chance." Furthermore, "If doctors ever recommend that the plug be pulled, I have ten people named in my will that either don't like each other or that would never agree with one another out of stubborn pride...or spite. And, in order for that plug to be pulled, the decision would have to be unanimous."

Marvin's Gifts of Warmth

Marvin, while a shrewd business man, and fairly frugal when it came to material things, was very giving. Not in an extravagant sense, but in a practical sense. Some of his fondest memories as a child were of his mother bundling him up from the cold Brooklyn winters. He felt the love radiate from his mother as she lovingly, tenderly, and carefully made sure he was protected from the elements.

Marvin used to say those moments resonated with him and made him feel so loved that the feelings never faded. Because those memories were so deeply engrained in Marvin, he would give gifts of warmth to his friends. Many a holiday season I would visit Marvin and he would have gifts wrapped or in gift bags with name tags identifying the lucky recipient, strewn throughout his house.

Sometimes a few of the gifts would sit for several months. Marvin didn't mind, he knew the warmth and excitement of seeing someone receive his gift was worth the wait. You could see the joy in his face. Now, whenever I wear any of the items Marvin gave me throughout the years, I can't help but feel an emotional attachment, and affection, towards Marvin.

Journey to Ken Rotcop's Workshop

Ken Rotcop holds two writing workshops a week for aspiring and seasoned writers—one at his home in Woodland Hills, California, and one at the Farmer's Market in Los Angeles. Marvin Kaplan and I attended the workshop at Ken's home on Tuesday nights from 7 to 10pm. In fact, *Lookin' Up* is one of the scripts Marvin and I wrote while in the workshop. The film was in the final steps of post-production when we lost Marvin in 2016.

Our trip to Ken's house was quite the ordeal, slowed by the increased immobility Marvin was experiencing as the years took their toll. Ultimately, Marvin was heavily dependent on a wheelchair, and getting him to and from the workshop became too difficult. Still, I wouldn't trade that time together with Marvin for anything.

My normal hours of work at my Warner Bros. job were 8 to 5. On Tuesday's I'd work 7 - 4; that extra hour was needed to get Marvin to class on time. Arriving to Marvin's house by 5, we'd spend the next hour getting ready for the drive to Ken's house.

I'd gather all of Marvin's notes for the project we were working on, combine them with mine, and put them into Marvin's backpack. He'd have half a dozen other projects in the bag that he insisted on bringing with him, making the bag exceptionally heavy.

Marvin, being from New York, dressed in layers—and he was a master at it. Even, what was to me, a hot night would require a couple of layers of clothing, including almost always a sweater. Generally, Marvin knows what he wants to wear, but finding the right combination of layers was the key. Watching him mix and match articles of clothing was like watching a woman try on dress after dress, looking for just the right one. I don't mean to sound like I'm stereotyping women, but you get the point. Once all the layers are in place, he'd add a scarf and a herringbone cap, usually his grey one.

I'd help Marvin to his feet and support him as he walked to the door, with a cane, and with great trepidation. He'd take the small step over the threshold and hold the rail he had installed on his porch. I'd take his key ring, which contained more than 60 keys, and use the only key for locking the door. Offering to "get rid of" the keys that no longer served a purpose was like asking Marvin to give up snacks—it wasn't going to happen. Fortunately, I finally figured out how to identify the key I needed, but never understood his fixation on having a cluttered key ring. I hated that key ring!

Once Marvin was in the car and seat belted in, we'd drive to Woodland Hills. I loved the drive! Sure, it was rush hour traffic, but Marvin never ran out of stories to share. We'd talk about the script we were working on, or another project he was working on, or he'd sing me some of the new songs he'd written for one of his plays. And if something interesting was happening in the news, he'd have something to say about it. Through the years we discussed politics, religion, life, death, love, new story ideas, and a whole lot more, all while driving to and from Ken's writer's workshop.

Once in Woodland Hills, and before going to the workshop, we'd stop by Burger King. Every week I treated Marvin to a hot apple turnover and a carton of milk to "hold him over" through the workshop. Every so often Marvin would "remind me" to stop at Burger King...as if he needed to.

We'd arrive early at Ken's house so that we could get the first or second spot in Ken's driveway. Since the driveway was on an incline, it was important to get Marvin as close to the front door as possible. Marvin would eat his pie and drink his milk before venturing into the house. Once inside the house, Marvin would take off his shoes and make his way to the bathroom. By the time we made it to the living room, most of the other students had arrived. Marvin would sit in one of the arm chairs. I'd set out our notes, put his cane in the corner, and load him up with snacks so graciously provided by Ken and his wife, Connie. Connie was wise to move her breakable things out of Marvin's reach. Marvin wasn't clumsy, the precaution was like that taken when a toddler is around knickknacks.

I love it when Ken tells the stories of Marvin in the workshop, so I'm going to jump over that part and leave it to Ken.

On the ride home, Marvin and I would talk about the notes we'd received on our project, and about the projects that some of the other writers were working on. Marvin was quieter on the ride home, probably getting sleepy. But, on every single occasion, I would glance over and realize how good of a friend Marvin had been. There was something peaceful and comforting in those moments.

Once home and comfortably inside, Marvin would remove his scarf and his cap, and the layers of outdoor clothing. He'd beeline his way to his chair, an electric assisted recliner. Marvin would have me get him a snack, which would range from a left-over sandwich to a bowl of ice cream; from a piece of cake to a bowl of cereal. We'd review our writing goals for the coming week and call it a night. I'd usually get home around 11:30pm, exhausted, enlightened, and grateful to have Marvin Kaplan as a friend.

Katherine Hepburn on Marvin Kaplan

Everyone knows that Katherine Hepburn discovered Marvin Kaplan. If ever there was a turning point that identified Marvin's path, it was likely that. Marvin loved being an actor and he loved other actors. Once, several years ago, I watched as Marvin paid the dues for several actors who had fallen behind in their dues with the theatre they belonged to. I was so touched that I wrote a letter to Katherine Hepburn.

In the letter, I'd mentioned how fortunate the world is to have a man like Marvin Kaplan; a man who truly loves his craft and respects those with the same fervor as he possesses. I thanked her for her discovery.

Her response—which surprised me to receive—was simple, yet it resonates with me. It said:

Dear Steven Carter,
Marvin Kaplan is a lovely man but he gives me far too much credit. He is a very talented actor.
Thank you for your kind words.
(signed)
Katherine Hepburn

✖ ✖ ✖

Mary Cobb taught at the New York Film Academy.
Two Gentlemen
I was teaching a class on Shakespeare for the New York Film Academy when the topic of the comics in *Two Gentlemen of Verona* came up, and my students wondered how one would play the comic characters. In a modern style, or in some pastiche of Renaissance acting?

Only a day later, I had luncheon with my friend, Steven Carter, and I mentioned that question about comedy. And Steven suggested that Marvin Kaplan come to speak to my NYFA students on comedy and how to play it in films, television, or in Shakespearean plays. It was a wonderful idea, and we enjoyed three hours wherein Marvin described his life in theatre and film; where he taught the students simply by example, how to play a laugh line; how to intrigue and delight the audience by turns; how to be inspired by the material and your fellow actors.

Steven and he also spoke on writing for film and how comedy can be written to ensure a laugh (see Neil Simon). It was a wealthy few hours, and the students were amazed, delighted, and appreciated Marvin's and Steven's enthusiasm and great finesse in the industry.

Giving back is a long-standing tradition in the theatre, and Marvin and Steven gave back so much that day. Those of us who live our lives in the theatre understand that the process is threefold: apprentice, journeyman, and master. Marvin was in the latter category. An inspired actor. A reticent man of charm and discernment. A "Launce" who could make us laugh or cry as he determined.

It was a privilege to get to know Marvin, even peripherally. His longtime friend and writing partner, Steven Carter, was his great and good friend to the literal end. Steven is the kind of friend we all want: loyal, gracious, and steadfast. The quote below is for both of these men; two great friends and masters of comedy. But mostly, for Marvin.

> "Come, gentle night, come loving black-browed night, give
> Me my Romeo. And when he shall die,
> Take him and cut him out in little stars.
> And he will make the face of heaven so fine
> That all the world will be in love with night
> And pay no worship to the garish sun."

A Footnote Regarding Mary Cobb's Contribution by Steven Carter

We were guest speakers for Mary's class. Before the class started, and the students were filing in, one could sense that Mary is the type of instructor that we've all had one like in our lifetime; the one that resonates with us always. Each of Mary's students introduced themselves to Marvin and me. By the time they'd finished with introductions, I was fortunate enough to remember Marvin's name, Mary's name, my own name, and a couple of the student's names.

Marvin remembered them all. That's amazing, but it didn't surprise me, because that was something I'd seen Marvin do many times before. There was a scheduling mix up on the classroom, so we were moved to another classroom.

The students, naturally, entered the new room sitting randomly throughout the room and not in the same order as when the introductions were made. Marvin still remembered every one of their names, and even referenced something they shared about themselves in his response. That's a gift, a true talent! It's an "awe" factor that we'll always remember.

✖ ✖ ✖

The Red Skelton Show

Here's a funny story that writer Julio Martinez passed on about Marvin.

One of Marvin's favorite shows to be a guest on was the Red Skelton Show. Red was a funny man, but never funnier than when he did rehearsals, because he would ad-lib dirty lines throughout the rehearsal. Lines like "She wants to play tennis. I just want her to use my balls." Or, "She wants a lollypop. Well, she can suck my lollypop any time she wants." I think you get the idea.

So, when they were actually doing the show, anytime it came to a part in the script where Marvin would remember Red's dirty ad-libs, Marvin would break up, and the audience laughed along not knowing the real reason Marvin was laughing and why Red had a smirk on his face!

✖ ✖ ✖

From Doug West, one of Marvin's traveling companions.

The Theater, Always the Theater

Marvin and I traveled to Paris and London together in June, 1984. The flight was a charter out of LAX that was scheduled to leave at 4pm but, instead it left at the most glorious hour of 4am. Needless to say, upon arrival we had more than the usual case of jet lag. The next day we were still hurting, but Marvin, as tired as he was, wanted to go to a matinee in the West End of London.

The play was called *Daisy Pulls It Off*. Marvin and I were doing pretty good through the intermission. However, that all changed in the second half.

It was not the most exciting play, and Marvin was fighting to stay awake. Well, I was paying attention to the play when it got to a rather quiet part and I heard a noise. A long loud noise that went throughout the theater.

There was no way the actors on stage didn't hear it either, as we were sitting up close to the stage, and the same went for everybody in the theater. Marvin was sitting a few seats away from me and I turned to ask him what the noise was. One look and I knew what it was.

It was Marvin's snoring that was being heard all over the theater. After the show, I asked him what he thought of the play. He rolled his eyes back and said the play should be renamed *Daisy Sleeps It Off*.

✖ ✖ ✖

Mark Evanier is a TV writer and producer of the animated show *Garfield*. He remembers this story about Marvin.

Working Garfield

"Well, it's sort of about Marvin. He's in it, anyway. But first, it's about the kind of agent who gives that profession a bad name. I used to write and voice direct the CBS Saturday morning animated series *Garfield and Friends*. It was one of the best jobs I ever had, in part because once we started getting decent ratings, I was granted a lot of power and control. I had a great relationship with Jim Davis, creator and controller of *Top Cat*. I also had a great relationship with the folks over at the network.

The second of these is the impressive one. Everyone who's worked with Jim for any length of time has had a good relationship with him. A good relationship with the execs at a major television network...ah, that's not so common. Basically though, I could write whatever I wanted—within reason. And I could cast any actor I wanted to have do voices—within budget. We had a set fee we paid our guest actors, and only a few people I tried to hire were not fine with that amount.

This gave me the opportunity to engage actors whose work I'd always loved, and many of those actors had appeared in my favorite movie, *It's a Mad, Mad, Mad, Mad World*. Among the thespians who appeared in *Mad World* and who also did at least one episode of *Garfield and Friends* were, Jonathan Winters, Buddy Hackett, Stan Freberg, Arnold Stang, Don Knotts, Lennie Weinrib, Jesse White...and Marvin Kaplan. As our story begins, I had yet to hire Marvin, though I certainly intended to. I just hadn't gotten around yet to writing an episode with a Marvin Kaplan type character in it.

I had, however, just written a script with a role for another actor who had a small part in *Mad World*. For the purposes of this story, he shall remain nameless. I found out who his agent was, called the man, explained what we wanted and when we wanted him and what we paid. The agent tried to dicker with me over the money, but I stopped him. I said, "This is what we pay for this kind of role and it's been fine with dozens of other actors over the years we've been on the air. I'm afraid it's take-it-or-leave-it. I'm not empowered to go any higher."

The agent called his client, then called me back and they accepted. Something seemed a bit odd to me about the agent's attitude, so after we hung up, I faxed him a memo confirming our agreement. It stated the amount we'd be paying, the name of the studio where we were recording and its address, the call time, etc. We would be recording the following Tuesday.

I assumed everything was set. I assumed wrongly.

Monday evening at 6:05pm, the agent called me and said, "I believe you wanted my client tomorrow at 9am. Let's firm up what you're paying him." I looked at the clock, saw what time it was, and knew exactly what was happening.

I said, "We're paying him the amount you and I agreed upon, which is the same amount I put down in the fax I sent you shortly after our last phone conversation." The agent denied ever receiving a fax from me and denied that he'd agreed to any dollar figure. If we didn't settle on one now, his client was not showing up the next morning at nine.

If you haven't figured out the 6:05 part yet, allow me to explain. Agencies close at various times, but most are closed by 6:00. He was hoping that it was too late for me to call another agency and book someone else. He was further hoping that not having someone to play that role at 9am would screw up my recording session and cause me enough problems that I'd agree there and then to a higher amount.

I told him what the job paid. He told me that amount was an insult to his client, who never worked for that kind of money. I named some actors who were much bigger stars than his client who'd been on the show working for that money. He told me his client was a much bigger star than any of them, which was not even close to true. He told me what I'd have to pay to have his client there the next morning. I told him I wasn't permitted to pay above the price I'd cited and I said, "If your client doesn't work for that kind of money, he doesn't work for that kind of money. I'll go find someone who does." End of call.

This was not all that gutsy on my part. I knew a dozen actors well enough that I could call them at home if I couldn't reach their agents just then. I could also rearrange the schedule for the next day's recording session and move the 9am episode to later in the day. That would give me time to call another agency in the morning and book someone else to be there in the afternoon.

But I didn't have to do that because I immediately phoned Paul Doherty, the man I considered the best, smartest voiceover agent in the business. It was 6:15, and Paul was still in his office. His secretary had left so he answered his phone himself. "An agent with a lot less ethics than you has just tried to pull the 6:05pm trick on me," I told him. He knew exactly what I was talking about. "Who have you got who might not be working tomorrow morning?"

Paul read off a list of about ten names and I probably could have hired any of them...but when he got to Marvin Kaplan, I decided he was perfect. Paul knew what we paid and had the integrity to abide by an oral agreement...so when he said, "Great. I'll have Marvin there at nine," I knew Marvin would be there at nine. Actually, he was there at eight, but I'll get to that. First, I have to tell you that at 6:25pm that same evening, the agent for the other guy in *Mad World*—the one who didn't work for what we paid— called me back.

He said, "I've got to apologize. I looked next to the fax machine and I found the fax you sent the other day. It must've fallen out of the machine and behind the stand, and on it, you did specify the amount. My client never works for this kind of money, but I just talked it over with him and we both feel that since there was this confusion and part of it was my fault for not noticing the fax earlier and calling you, we should make an exception this one time."

I said, "That's very decent of you, but you don't need to make that sacrifice. I've already booked someone else. Please tell your client I very much admire his work and I'm sorry we won't be working together." The agent did not sound happy.

Now as you probably already know, Marvin had a lot of trouble with his eyes. He showed up at the recording session an hour early, hoping that he could get his script and study it so that he wouldn't make too many mistakes. One of the marks of a true professional is that he or she does everything possible to not cause problems for their employers and co-workers, and Marvin was very much a professional. In fact, he was a professional with a big magnifying glass with which he hoped to go over the script we would give him.

The problem was that I wasn't there at 8am. No one was except our producer, Bob Nesler, who had piles of the nine scripts we'd be recording that day. Marvin asked him if he could have a copy of the script he was in...and since Bob didn't know which one that was, he gave Marvin a stack containing all nine. Marvin reportedly reacted in horror to all that paper. Then he scurried off and found an empty office in the studio and began reading them all, trying to find the Marvin Kaplan role.

A little before nine, I arrived for the session and all the other actors strolled in. By 9:05, we had everyone but Marvin. I knew he was a pro, so I decided to wait for him rather than start on some other script. When he hadn't shown at 9:15, I called his agency and a junior agent there told me he'd been given the proper call time and it was quite unlike Marvin to be late.

At 9:30, I told Nesler I'd decided to start on some other script since Marvin Kaplan was late. He said, "Oh, Marvin's not late. He's been here since eight o'clock."

I quickly searched the studio and found Marvin sitting at a desk in an empty office, looking panicky as he paged through script after script with his magnifying glass, trying to learn every part that might have been his. I greeted him and showed him which role it was and he said, "Oh, I was afraid of that. That character has an awful lot of lines and I don't see very well and..."

I pulled out a script I'd printed out just for him. It had VERY LARGE TYPE, and I asked him, "Will this help?"

He flipped through it, gave me a big grin and said, "Mr. DeMille... I'm ready for my close-up."

We recorded that script in the usual amount of time. Marvin took two or three takes for a few lines, but not many. His first reading was almost always perfect, and I was kinda glad that the other guy had uncast himself the way he did.

Hey, wanna see it? You'll have to hurry because I'm linking to an egregious copyright violation, and at this very moment, lawyers are probably doing whatever it is one does to get something yanked from YouTube. But if it's still there, you can enjoy Marvin Kaplan in the title role of "Angel Puss"...

Wasn't he great? If his voice hadn't been so distinctive, I wouldn't have felt I had to wait a while before hiring him again to play a different character.

There's actually more to this story, but it doesn't involve Marvin. A few days after the recording session, the agent for the actor who didn't work for what we paid called and told me his client would work for what we paid. "He really likes your show and wants to be a part of it," said the agent.

I didn't know if the client was complicit in the last-minute extortion or if it was just the agent trying to up his commission money and show off for the actor. I decided to give the actor the benefit of the doubt. After all, he was good at what he did and he was in *It's a Mad, Mad, Mad, Mad World*. So I said, "I don't have anything now, but the next time I write a role that I think suits him, I'll give you a call."

Some months later, I did. I called the agent, reminded him of the fee we paid and we made a verbal deal. I faxed him another memo, and this time, he phoned me back to acknowledge receipt and to say his client would be in the proper place at the proper time. You can probably guess what happened when my phone rang at 6:05pm—of all times!—the night before that recording session.

This time, it was: "There was some misunderstanding between my client and me. I know I agreed to the money and I thought he had...but I just called to remind him of the call time and he asked me what the job paid. When I told him, he said, 'I won't do it. That's less than I've ever gotten before!' and...well, I think I can get him to show up if you could just give me a little help in the money department here. Just a 50% bump, that's all. That's still way less than he got for a job last week..."

I said, "Let me put you on hold for a minute." I put him on hold, called Paul Doherty and asked him who he had who was available the next day. Paul said, "How about Buddy Hackett? He was in here a half-hour ago asking me to get him more animation work." I said I'd take him, and then I went back to the non-ethical agent and told him, "Your client is off the hook. I just booked Buddy Hackett for the money your guy won't work for. You know Buddy Hackett. The guy who's on with Johnny Carson tonight and who's headlining at Caesars Palace in Vegas starting Friday? Bye!"

And of course, Buddy Hackett was fine. He was a very funny man, and he even told me and the rest of the cast and crew a number of great dirty jokes. He was also a much bigger star than the sleazy agent's client, plus Buddy was one of the major stars of *It's a Mad, Mad, Mad, Mad World*, as opposed to the guy he replaced on our show, who was a bit player in the film. I think that alone makes the end of this whole story just about perfect.

✖ ✖ ✖

Bonnie Janofsky was Marvin's musical collaborator.
Music by Janofsky, Lyrics by Kaplan
Bonnie Janofsky was Marvin's composer for the movies he produced and the musicals he wrote. For eighteen years they worked together. In fact, they met in a musical theater workshop in 1999 and almost immediately teamed up, she writing the music, Marvin the lyrics.

And through the years, she watched his body begin to break down.

He loved eating but hated exercising. Bonnie wondered how Marvin could drive, his eyesight was so bad. They would work at her house. He inevitable drove past the house because he couldn't see. In parking lots it took him hours to find his car. He was truly Mr. Magoo.

In later years, photos of Marvin showed him with one eye, his right eye, partially or completely closed.

He told Bonnie how that came to be.

"For the longest time I put off having cataract surgery," he told her. "I knew my eyesight wasn't good, but I didn't like the idea of someone fooling around with my eyes."

"But, finally, after a lot of close calls, near accidents, and some scraping of sides of cars and tires, I figured it was time.

"They gave me anesthesia which knocked me out and prepared me for surgery.

"Only I woke up just as the scalpel was coming for my eye! I jerked my head. He stuck my eye."

Marvin lost the vision in that eye.

Years later, he was forced to have cataract surgery in the left eye or he would have been legally blind. He did, but with a different doctor, different hospital.

Bonnie collected dozens of Marvin-stories over the years but the following is her favorite:

Marvin said, "I was doing a play out of town somewhere. I forget where. It ran for a number of weeks and my understudy was getting impatient because he had never gone on.

"One day at rehearsal I coughed. I just had a tickle in my throat. One lousy cough!

"The understudy, backstage, saw his chance. He called 911, said it was an emergency. An ambulance came over and, despite my protesting, took me away!

"The understudy, bless his heart, went on in my place.

"I could've killed him!" said Marvin with that he-haw laugh that he had.

✖ ✖ ✖

Jack Sehres became Marvin's young driver and pal.

Driving Mr. Kaplan

Marvin came into my life through my parents, the Holts, and Theatre West.

I was told an older gentleman needed a driver and an assistant. Little did I know at the time what an impact this older gentleman would have on my life, from the pure entertainment factor of his stories to the wisdom of a generation often forgotten by mine.

I have many memories of the years I spent driving, talking, and helping Marvin. From hilarious issues of parking while using a wheelchair, to trying to communicate with someone hard of hearing...

One time I arrived to pick him up and he had just gotten new hearing aids. So he starts telling me (yelling to me), "Jack come here. Can you help me with these damn things? I can't get the batteries in with my fat fingers." I did my best to help get the batteries in, and then stood and watched as he was attempting to put them in his ears himself. Eventually he asked for my help, and we succeeded in putting them in. This was one of my favorite characteristics of Marvin—he was stubborn and steadfast in his beliefs, especially in situations that illustrated what he felt he could still do; from acting, to eating, to handling his own hearing aids.

Many times while I was "working," we would just hang out and talk. We had constant conversations about politics, what was messed up and how through all the generations the same issues persisted. Marvin's sharp, dark, and dry sense of humor was visible through everything, never missing a beat, always finding something funny, even within the darkest truths. One day I was helping Marvin copyright one of his plays. Without getting too far into the plot line, it was basically a comedy about a guy losing it in our crazy, modern world and killing people in the media because of the frenzy that they create.

Now keep in mind, conversations with Marvin were at best two thirds Marvin talking, one third you sharing, and all of it half translated because of the lack of hearing. Through it all, the hearing aids did little to nothing. However, this issue of hearing just added to the color of Marvin's personality and his ability to stay confident and entertaining, while being disabled.

For one of our many adventures, Marvin asked me to take him to the AIDS benefit concert, and on the way we would pick up one of his friends... Connie Sawyer, another legend, and also hard of hearing. Both worked during the same era and had a lot to talk about. So imagine, Marvin in the front seat, Connie in the back seat, and me driving.

They're both talking (yelling) at each other, only to hear every other word the other has said. They would also then elaborate over one another on two separate topics, with a vigor matched by none.

They would start on an old movie they had been in, or a friend they both knew, and from there it would just go on and on, both speaking extremely fast, on two separate topics, only sometimes catching another name they both knew, to then launch into two separate monologues about old gags they had done, or episodes of a TV show they had been in, or the scenes from the movies, plays, or the other countless things and actors Connie and Marvin both knew.

This vocal sharing time went on from The Motion Picture home all the way to the theatre, a good 45 minutes. I got a couple of words in, or would help relay the message at some points, but for the most part, I got to just enjoy the stories they both had to share.

The amount of time and work they had both seen and done was astounding to me. While being brought up by actors who love the classics aided me in talking about old movies and plays, I was still ignorant to the vast majority that were made.

Marvin enlightened me on many old movies, tv shows, and plays. By the time Marvin finished apprising me of plots in different mediums, I was sold. I knew the story and everyone involved in it and on it. Being the age I am, (23), hanging and working with Marvin and his friends really pushed me in my knowledge of old movies and plays, both things I now enjoy.

Over time, working with Marvin became working for a friend. We had our routine. Half the time we were seeing movies, or eating a meal at one of his favorite Hollywood restaurants.

On a normal day, I would go to work for Marvin having no idea what we were going to do that day.

On one occasion, we went to the reunion event of *It's a Mad, Mad, Mad, Mad World*. There was a red carpet, a bunch of press, and Marvin was in his element. He was funny and charming. I, however, was standing behind Marvin's wheelchair super awkward, wondering what I'm doing there! Pictures being snapped from every angle, people staring, others asking for his autograph. It was crazy.

To top it off, I was wearing a t-shirt... After a while I got used to the nature of Marvin's "appointments" and dressed in business casual. Marvin liked to wear his sweatsuit with a sweater. I don't think he varied from there.

Working for and with Marvin was a joy, and one of the best jobs I have ever had. I will definitely carry his stories, and his tenacity, with me from here on out. He will be missed by many.

He will be missed by me.

✳ ✳ ✳

Gabriella Carteris, President of Screen Actors Guild-American Federation of Television and Radio Artists.

Following Marvin's Death

"Marvin was the face that everyone recognized. He was your kindly neighbor, your favorite uncle or, as he was on the sitcom *Alice*, a 'regular guy' phone company employee and the favorite coffee shop customer. Marvin was one of the most recognizable character actors of his generation, and he was a proud union activist and leader. We are forever grateful for the gift of his work and his service to our members.

"He had a lifelong career in film, television, radio, commercials, and animation.

"He made his TV debut in 1953 as a co-star of the comedy series *Meet Millie*, and beside *Alice*, appeared in popular TV programs through the next four decades, including a recurring role on *Becker*, and guest appearances on *Charlie's Angels*, *CHiPS*, *ER*, *The Fall Guy*, *Gidget*, *Gomer Pyle: USMC*, *I Dream of Jeannie*, *Julia*, *Love American Style*, *MacGyver*, *McHale's Navy*, *The Mod Squad*, and *Petticoat Junction*. In 1978, he began a seven-year run as telephone repairman Henry Beesmire in the award-winning comedy *Alice*. Kaplan also added his unique comic touch to feature films like *The Great Race*, *Freaky Friday*, and *It's a Mad, Mad, Mad, Mad World*.

Marvin's voice became familiar to generations of children thanks to his work on *Top Cat, Garfield and Friends, Aaah!!! Real Monsters,* and *Johnny Bravo,* among others.

He was a playwright, a screenwriter, a proud union activist and leader, and most of all, a dedicated actor and a good friend.

He will be missed.

Watch Out for Slick

Marvin's parting shot to Hollywood was to write, produce, and finance two feature films using all his old friends and colleagues.

"The nice thing about growing old," he once told the writers in my workshop, "is that you can do whatever you want."

And so, at the age of 87, Marvin put all the pieces together for what he called a gray comedy, *Watch Out for Slick*.

Slick was this old, lazy dog that stretched out and slept across the front door, so whenever anyone was coming in or going out, the owner would caution, "*Watch out for Slick*." Hence, the title.

But the story was actually about an old-timer who marries this gorgeous, much younger maiden who is kidnapped and held for a ransom, much more money than the old-timer has.

All the neighbors are willing to help out the old husband, except his wife has really not been kidnapped, she's run off with her young, dashing boyfriend, and the two of them are trying to scam the old-timer.

The script was cute, funny, and endearing.

Marvin said he got the idea for the story from his neighborhood in Brooklyn.

"There were kidnappings all the time," he said.

"Slick is based on true-life experiences. But, where in real life kidnapping was a tragedy, in my story I turn it into a farce. I knew I could write it funny, but that's not why I produced it. I produced it for the actors I had worked with and socialized with, most of them for over 50 or 60 years.

Nowadays, most movie stars are young, good looking actors. Nothing wrong with that, but where are parts for the seniors? The ones who have worked at their craft for half-a-century?

"I also wanted to write a warm, fuzzy, simple story about older, decent people. People you could identify with, people you could laugh with, not at, people you could care about."

The average age of his cast was over 70, including actress Connie Sawyer, who claimed she was a born in 1912. (You figure it out.)

Marvin felt this talent pool of senior actors and actresses was being over looked in today's market. He hoped that Slick would give them the visibility to open the eyes of other writers and producers.

They shot *Slick* in 15 days, unheard of for a feature.

Marvin told why. "These senior actors arrive on time, there are no primadonnas, they know their lines, and they bring great enthusiasm to the set. And they're good!"

Marvin ended with, "It's time for Hollywood to turn the other cheek—to the one that's wrinkled."

Looking Up

Now 88 years old, Marvin had one more comedy up his clown's sleeve. Again, writing, producing, and financing, Marvin created another zany, dark comedy with lovable characters.

Looking Up is about a bank teller who day dreams about some day being famous, so famous that he would be on television regularly and would be beloved by the nation.

And then calamity hits the fan. He loses his job, his wife is having an affair, his mother-in-law drives him crazy, and his daughter has sold his beloved dog.

When he sees a serial killer on television being interviewed on all the magazines and talk shows, he plots how he can kill two birds with one stone, knock off his family and become a TV celebrity.

When the house accidentally blows up and wife, mother-in-law, and daughter are killed, the former bank teller is falsely accused of murdering them. Does he cry out his innocence? Of course not. He's now a TV celebrity. *Sixty Minutes* wants him. So does *20/20*. And *The View* and *Oprah* and *Howard Stern*, and on and on.

Marvin's weird sense of humor at work!

The movie starred the veteran comedy actor Steve Guttenberg as the forlorn bank teller.

Guttenberg, talking about the film in *Daily Variety* said, "I think Marvin's script is wonderful in terms of portraying the absurdity of modern life."

Unfortunately, Marvin passed away before the film was finished.

BEFORE WE ROLL THE END CREDITS

All of Marvin's incredible credits, minus the theater credits, are listed on the following page.

It was not my intent to write about all the shows he did, or all the performances he gave, or all his activities beyond acting. I'll leave that to someone else.

I just wanted to share with you the man, who he was, who some of his friends were, and some of his accomplishments in a career that only ended by his death.

Anyone whose life he touched knew him as a friend, an uncle, a mentor, an enthusiastic fan of good acting, good movies, good theater, and good food.

As I said in the opening, if this book sounded like a love letter, it's because it is.

FADE OUT

THE END

Marvin Kaplan's List of Credits

Lookin' Up
Vic Greeley
2016

Watch Out for Slick
2015

Cinerama Dome's 50th Anniversary Celebration (Video short)
2008-2013

The Garfield Show (TV Series)
Additional Voices
- Unpleasant Accordion Music (2013) ... Additional Voices (voice)
- Super Me/Mastermind (2009) ... Additional Voices (voice)
- A Game of Cat and Mouse/Perfect Pizza (2009) ... Additional Voices (voice)
- Pasta Wars/Mother Garfield (2009) ... Additional Voices (voice)
- The Pizza Tron 7000 (2008) ... Additional Voices (voice)
2012

Autism and Cake (Short)
Mark
2009

Dark and Stormy Night
Gunny
2005

McBride: The Chameleon Murder (TV Movie)
Mr. Bernard
1998-2004

Becker (TV Series)
Mr. Gordon
- DNR (2004) ... Mr. Gordon
- Trials and Defibrillations (2001) ... Mr. Gordon
- Truth and Consequences (1999) ... Mr. Gordon

- Man Plans, God Laughs (1998) ... Mr. Gordon
2002

Even Stevens (TV Series)
Old Guy #1
- Boy on a Rock (2002) ... Old Guy #1
1999

ER (TV Series)
Kornberg's Father
- Sticks and Stones (1999) ... Kornberg's Father
1997

Johnny Bravo (TV Series)
Woody
- Going Batty/Berry the Butler/Red Faced in the White House
  (1997) ... Woody (voice)
1996

Aaahh!!! Real Monsters (TV Series)
Skeech / Sculptor
- Eye Full of Wander/Lifestyles of the Rich and Scary (1996) ...
  Skeech / Sculptor (voice)
1995

The Cartoon Cartoon Show (TV Series)
Dave D. Fly
- O. Ratz: Rat in a Hot Tin Can (1995) ... Dave D. Fly (voice)
1994

Revenge of the Nerds IV: Nerds in Love (TV Movie)
Mr. Dawson
1993

The Big Gig (Short)
1993

Witchboard 2
Morris
1992

Monster in My Pocket: The Big Scream (TV Short)
Vampire (voice)
1992

On the Air (TV Series)
Dwight McGonigle
- Episode #1.7 (1992) ... Dwight McGonigle
- Episode #1.6 (1992) ... Dwight McGonigle
- Episode #1.5 (1992) ... Dwight McGonigle
- Episode #1.4 (1992) ... Dwight McGonigle
- Episode #1.3 (1992) ... Dwight McGonigle
Show all 7 episodes
1991

Garfield and Friends (TV Series)
Angel Puss
- Moo Cow Mutt/Big Bad Buddy Bird/Angel Puss (1991) ... Angel
  Puss (voice)
1991

Delirious
Typewriter Repairman
1991

They Came from Outer Space (TV Series)
Dr. Kendall
- The Legend (1991) ... Dr. Kendall
1990

Monsters (TV Series)
Murray Van Pelt
- Murray's Monster (1990) ... Murray Van Pelt
1990

Wake, Rattle & Roll (TV Series)
Choo Choo (1990) (voice)
1990

Wild at Heart
Uncle Pooch
1989

Double Your Pleasure (TV Movie)
Jeff
1989

My Two Dads (TV Series)
Burnin' Vernon McCracken
- Playing with Fire (1989) ... Burnin' Vernon McCracken
1989

The Further Adventures of SuperTed (TV Series)
Man at Radio Station
- Phantom of the Grand Ol' Opry (1989) ... Man at Radio Station
  (voice)
1988

1st & Ten: The Championship (TV Series)
Irv
- Team Picture (1988) ... Irv
1988

Cagney & Lacey (TV Series)
Jerrold Plotnik
- A Fair Shake: Part 1 (1988) ... Jerrold Plotnik
1988

Top Cat and the Beverly Hills Cats (TV Movie)
Choo-Choo (voice)
1986

The Smurfs (TV Series)
Additional Voices
- Smurfquest: Part 1/Smurfquest: Part 2 (1986) ... Additional
  Voices (voice)
1986

The Fall Guy (TV Series)
Joe
- The Bigger They Are (1986) ... Joe
1986

MacGyver (TV Series)
The Chess Master

- A Prisoner of Conscience (1986) ... The Chess Master
1986

Hollywood Vice Squad
Man with doll
1978-1985

Alice (TV Series)
Henry
- Th-th-th-that's All Folks (1985) ... Henry
- Kiss the Grill Goodbye (1985) ... Henry
- Tommy's Lost Weekend (1984) ... Henry
- Space Sharples (1984) ... Henry
- Mel Spins His Wheels (1984) ... Henry
Show all 82 episodes
1981-1984

ABC Weekend Specials (TV Series)
Mouser / Sutcliffe
- Bad Cat (1984) ... Mouser (voice)
- Arthur the Kid (1981) ... Sutcliffe
1984

Don't Ask Me, Ask God (TV Movie)
Neighbor #1
1983

Deck the Halls with Wacky Walls (TV Movie)
Stick'um (voice)
1983

Saturday Supercade (TV Series)
Shellshock 'Shelly' Turtle
- The Who-Took-Toadwalker Story//Banana Bikers/Disc Derby
  Fiasco/Rocky Mountain Monkey Business(1983) ... Shellshock
  'Shelly' Turtle (voice)
- Gorilla Gangster/Sheep Rustle Hustle/Spaced Out Frogs/Ama-
  zon Jungle Bungle (1983) ... Shellshock 'Shelly' Turtle (voice)

- The Ms. Fortune Story/Mississippi Madness/Trucknapper
  Caper/Pitfall's Panda Puzzle (1983) ... Shellshock 'Shelly' Turtle
  (voice)
1980

Midnight Madness
Bonaventure Desk Clerk
1979

Flying High (TV Series)
Cutler
- Ladies of the Night (1979) ... Cutler
1978

CHiPs (TV Series)
Hilmer Nelson
- Disaster Squad (1978) ... Hilmer Nelson
1977

We've Got Each Other (TV Series)
Milton
- Miss Wonderful (1977) ... Milton
1977

Charlie's Angels (TV Series)
Zobar
- Circus of Terror (1977) ... Zobar
1977

C B Bears (TV Series)
Skids (voice)
1976

Freaky Friday
Carpet Cleaner
1975

The Lost Saucer (TV Series)
Scientist #1
- Get a Dorse (1975) ... Scientist #1
1974

Snakes
Brother Joy
1974

Kolchak: The Night Stalker (TV Series)
Delgado
- Bad Medicine (1974) ... Delgado
1974

Chopper One (TV Series)
Harry
- The Informer (1974) ... Harry
1972-1973

Love, American Style (TV Series)
The Psychiatrist (segment "Love and the Stutter") / Arnold (segment "Love and the Latin Lover")
- Love and the Games People Play/Love and High Spirits/Love and
   the Memento/Love and the Single Husband/Love and the Stutter (1973) ... The Psychiatrist (segment "Love and the Stutter")
- Love and the Bachelor Party/Love and the Latin Lover/Love
   and the Old-Fashioned Father/Love and the Test of Manhood
   (1972) ... Arnold (segment "Love and the Latin Lover")
1973

The Severed Arm
Mad Man Herman
1972

Wait Till Your Father Gets Home (TV Series)
Norman
- Love Story (1972) ... Norman (voice)
1971

The Chicago Teddy Bears (TV Series)
Marvin
- Billy the Kid (1971) ... Marvin
- The Spy (1971) ... Marvin
- The Alderman (1971) ... Marvin
- Tender Loving Kindness (1971) ... Marvin
1971

Julia (TV Series)
Mr. Crocker
- Courting Time (1971) ... Mr. Crocker
1970

I Dream of Jeannie (TV Series)
Perkins
- One of Our Hotels Is Growing (1970) ... Perkins
1969

Mod Squad (TV Series)
Sol Alpert / Sol Albert
- In This Corner - Sol Alpert (1969) ... Sol Alpert
- Flight Five Doesn't Answer (1969) ... Sol Albert
1969

Petticoat Junction (TV Series)
Stanley
- The Other Woman (1969) ... Stanley
1969

My World and Welcome to It (TV Series)
Corp. Schultz
- Man Against the World (1969) ... Corp. Schultz
1968

Premiere (TV Series)
Ethel
- Out of the Blue (1968) ... Ethel
1968

My Three Sons (TV Series)
Joe
- Gossip, Incorporated (1968) ... Joe
1968

Gomer Pyle: USMC (TV Series)
Mr. Kendall
- The Carriage Waits (1968) ... Mr. Kendall
1966

Gidget (TV Series)
Jeff Tracy
- Don't Defrost the Alligator (1966) ... Jeff Tracy
1966

Honey West (TV Series)
Byron Manners
- The Fun-Fun Killer (1966) ... Byron Manners
1965

Hank (TV Series)
Dudley Cobb
- The Campus Caper (1965) ... Dudley Cobb
1965

The Great Race
Frisbee
1965

McHale's Navy (TV Series)
Kwazniak
- All Ahead, Empty (1965) ... Kwazniak
1964-1965

Valentine's Day (TV Series)
Pet Store Owner / Landlord
- The Man Who Shot the World (1965)
- The Baritone Canary (1964) ... Pet Store Owner
- Call Me No Cabs (1964) ... Landlord
1964

The Baileys of Balboa (TV Series)
Louie
- Wanna Buy a Hot Turkey? (1964) ... Louie
1963-1964

Vacation Playhouse (TV Series)
Marvin / Marv
- Hooray for Hollywood (1964) ... Marvin
- Maggie Brown (1963) ... Marv
1964

Bob Hope Presents the Chrysler Theatre (TV Series)
Alvin
- The Game with Glass Pieces (1964) ... Alvin
1963

It's a Mad Mad Mad Mad World
Irwin
1963

A New Kind of Love
Harry
1963

Maggie Brown (TV Movie)
Marvin
1963

The Nutty Professor
English Student
1961-1962

Top Cat (TV Series)
Choo Choo / Choo-Choo
- Dibble's Double (1962) ... Choo Choo (voice)
- Griswald (1962) ... Choo Choo (voice)
- Dibble Sings Again (1962) ... Choo Choo (voice)
- Dibble Breaks the Record (1962) ... Choo Choo
- The Con Men (1962) ... Choo Choo (voice)
Show all 30 episodes
1961

The Detectives (TV Series)
Irwin
- Hit and Miss (1961) ... Irwin
1961
The Many Loves of Dobie Gillis (TV Series)

Mr. Monty W. Milfloss
- The Second Childhood of Herbert T. Gillis (1961) ... Mr. Monty
   W. Milfloss
1961

Acapulco (TV Series)
- Bell's Half Acre (1961)
1960

Tom, Dick and Harry (TV Movie)
Harry Murphy
1960

M Squad (TV Series)
Arbogast
- A Gun for Mother's Day (1960) ... Arbogast
1960

Wake Me When It's Over
Hap Cosgrove
1959

Alcoa Theatre (TV Series)
Harry Cooper
- Tom, Dick, and Harry (1959) ... Harry Cooper
1956-1958

The Red Skelton Hour (TV Series)
Pvt. Alvin / Alfred Pinzmetal
- Valentine Day's Double Date (1958) ... Pvt. Alvin
- Valentine's Day Double Date (Original) (1956) ... Alfred Pinzmetal
1958

Make Room for Daddy (TV Series)
Oscar 'Evil Eye' Schultz
- The Honeymoon (1958) ... Oscar 'Evil Eye' Schultz
- Evil Eye Schultz (1958) ... Oscar 'Evil Eye' Schultz
1952-1955

Meet Millie (TV Series)
Alfred Prinzmetal
- The Wedding Day (1955) ... Alfred Prinzmetal
- Ruining New Job for Millie (1955) ... Alfred Prinzmetal
- Getting Millie and Junior Together (1955) ... Alfred Prinzmetal
- Day Before the Wedding (1955) ... Alfred Prinzmetal
- Episode #4.27 (1955) ... Alfred Prinzmetal

Show all 78 episodes
1954

Shower of Stars (TV Series)
W. Somerset Kaplan
- Premiere Show (1954) ... W. Somerset Kaplan
1953

General Electric Theater (TV Series)
Marvin
- The Marriage Fix (1953) ... Marvin
1953

The Ford Television Theatre (TV Series)
Marvin
- Double Exposure (1953) ... Marvin
1952

The Fabulous Senorita
Clifford Van Kunkle
1951

The Andrews Sisters (TV Movie)
1951

Angels in the Outfield
Timothy Durney
1951

Behave Yourself!
Max the Umbrella
1951

Criminal Lawyer
Sam Kutler
1951

The Fat Man
Pinkie (uncredited)
1951

I Can Get It for You Wholesale
Arnold Fisher
1950

Hollywood Theatre Time (TV Series)
- The Florence Bates Show (1950)
1950

The Reformer and the Redhead
Leon
1950

Key to the City
Francis - Newspaper Photographer (uncredited)
1950

Francis
First Medical Corps lieutenant (uncredited)
1949

Adam's Rib
Court Stenographer (uncredited)
1949

Theatre Credits

Only in America - Harry Golden/The Show Place
Little Shop of Horrors - Mushnik/Stage West, Calgary, Canada
Cash Flow - Marty/Tiffany Theatre
The Cherry Orchard - Gaev/Pan-Andreas Theatre (Dramalogue
   Award)
The Odd Couple - Felix/Jester Dinner Theatre, Mission Hills,
   California
God's Favorite - Sidney/Mickey Rooney Dinner Theatre, San
   Diego, California
Norma, Is That You? - Ben/Fiesta Dinner Theatre, San Diego,
   California
The Sunshine Boys - Al Lewis/Harlequin Dinner Theatre, Costa
   Mesa, California
Awake and Sing - Myron/Theatre Venture
Last of the Red-Hot Lovers - Barney/Tour: St. Louis, Indianapolis

The Dybbuk - Meyer/Mark Taper Forum

Next! - Marion/Theatre West

Uncle Vanya - Telegin/Mark Taper Forum/director Harold Clurman

Oklahoma! - Ali Hakim/Sacramento Music Circus/with Earl Holliman

Sound of Music - Max/Gruber-Gross Tour/with Barbara Eden

Can-Can - Boris/Theatre Under The Stars, Atlanta, Georgia

BIOGRAPHY

Ken Rotcop won the Writer's Guild Award, the Image Award, and the Neil Simon Award for writing and producing the movie, *For Us, the Living: The Story of Medgar Evers*, starring Laurence Fishburne. He was the former Creative Head of Embassy Pictures, Cannon TV, Trans World Productions and Hanna-Barbera.

He has written for every form of television including talk shows, game shows, political shows, a magic show, animation, and sitcoms.

Ken's book, *As I Remember It: My Fifty-Year Career As An Award Winning Writer, Producer And Studio Executive* was released in 2017 by BearManor.

His next book, "Remembering Monte Hall" will be produced by BearManor for release in 2019.

He currently lives in Woodland Hills, California with his wife Connie and their Yorkie, Kady.

He may be reached at pitchmart@gmail.com